Great tales and curiosities from "The Hawkeye State"

AMAZING IOWA

FEATURING

CAITLIN CLARK, THE "CROOKEDEST STREET IN THE WORLD," WORLD RECORD HICCUPS, AND IOWA'S OWN MUSIC MAN

Michelle Sprout Murray

Dedication

For all of my amazing family members who have listened to my stories, traveled all over with me, and possessed an unwavering belief in my potential.

Thanks especially to my husband, Marc, who is willing to try anything with me . . . no matter where we are!

Reedy Press
PO Box 5131
St. Louis, MO 63139
www.reedypress.com

Library of Congress Control Number: 2024949621

ISBN: 9781681065755

Images courtesy of Michelle Sprout Murray unless otherwise noted.

Printed in the United States of America
25 26 27 28 29   5 4 3 2

Contents

CHAPTER FOUR

CHAPTER FIVE

Acknowledgments

When I tried to narrow down the amazing stories about Iowa, I realized how difficult a job this would be. Everyone and every place certainly has a story worth telling! I wish I could have shared every one of them in this book. Hopefully, this will whet your appetite about the people, places, and events in this great state smack dab in the middle of our country.

Writing this book has been a labor of love, and I truly appreciate the passion and support for this project . . . even in the quick texts people have shared just to check in with me about "how my 'Amazing' book is going!"

Thanks to everyone who suggested story ideas to include. I am truly grateful for the time that so many of Iowa's public libraries took in sharing suggestions or words of wisdom. I hope to make several more trips around the state to share this finished project with you!

Thanks also to Iowa's museums, historical societies, and tourism offices for answering my questions and assisting me in finding the perfect photos for this collection of stories.

Thanks, Reedy Press, for asking me to write this book and for providing the best team of people I could ask for. Thanks to my future readers, who chose this book when there are so many others out there calling your name.

And finally, a million thank-yous wouldn't be enough for my family, who is always behind me every step of the way. From my mom, dad, and sister, who traveled near and far with me and instilled a love of traveling somewhere special each year on my summer birthday . . . to my husband, two sons, daughter-in-law, and son's girlfriend (Marc, Nic, Noah, Lauren, and Madi), who have had to excuse my absentmindedness more than usual as my thoughts were all over Iowa during the course of putting this book together . . . I am blessed with having a tribe who loves me unconditionally and believes in my potential. I love you more than words can say.

Introduction

For those of us who have called Iowa our home state for most of our lives—even though at times we may have entertained the thought of living elsewhere—this book is for you. For those people who may only have visited Iowa when they were passing through on the way to another state, this book is also for you. And for those of you who have never been to Iowa because you get it mixed up with Idaho and figure all that Iowa has to offer is corn, guess what? This book is meant for you, too!

I have lived in Iowa all my life, but I've also traveled extensively around the world. So many times people think the "grass is greener" elsewhere. It turns out my home state is pretty . . . well . . . amazing (thus the title), and I had a ball finding out more about the very place I thought held no more surprises after all this time.

For example, two astronauts had humble beginnings in Iowa. There's also a woman who championed women's suffrage all over the country and a man who wrote a musical about his tiny Iowa hometown that people in New York City flocked to see.

There are haunted places, sports heroes, and foods that will make you want to cross state lines to try. Miracles, legends, and the ordinary made extraordinary . . . this is what is amazing about Iowa.

Prepare to learn more about this state you won't want to fly over anymore. On one hand, we are "Iowa nice" and love to have you visit. On the other hand, we're also a little "Iowa stubborn" and prefer to keep things to ourselves. Iowans don't like to boast . . . but we are pretty proud of it here.

back into time in
scatine's first Maid-Rite.

Chapter One

Iowa Firsts

Iowa has had many firsts in the country, from an invention that made it possible for people to say, "It's the best thing since sliced bread" to one that cured headaches without upsetting the stomach in the process. People have started small, dreamed big, and achieved gargantuan tasks, even ones that led them out of the country . . . or the planet.

Iowans don't take "no" for an answer when something they believe in is at stake. If there's a problem, they'll find a solution. If there's a record, they'll break it. Maybe it's the Midwestern work ethic or the stick-to-it-iveness that their ancestors passed down to them. Whatever it is, an Iowan is hard-working, tenacious, and inventive, and these "firsts" in the state are a good representation of what can be done when no one is looking—or even when they are.

If you use a computer, eat at fast-food establishments, or exercise your right to vote, you can thank an Iowan. Whether the "first" was for the betterment of society or quite the opposite, Iowa has seen people come up with creative ideas and become the first in the state and/or nation in doing so.

First Robbery of a Moving Train

Jesse and Frank James around 1872. Courtesy of Wikimedia Commons

Think of any old-time train robbery you've seen on TV, and an image of men jumping on a moving train may come to mind. This isn't how the world's first robbery of a moving train happened, although it probably made for better TV viewing.

Jesse James and his band of outlaws learned that a train headed across the country was going to be carrying gold worth about $75,000 (in July 1873) and that the train was coming through Adair on the recently built main line of the Chicago, Rock Island & Pacific Railroad. Jesse sent his brother, Frank James, and Cole Younger to Omaha to find out when the shipment would arrive while he and several other outlaws stayed back in Adair concocting a plan to steal the gold. The problem was that the train would be moving, and they had to figure out a way to get on it.

Frank and Cole returned to Adair with the tip that the gold was on its way east. Jesse's plan was underway. First, some of the bandits obtained some food and pies from the wife of the section foreman to distract her while other bandits broke into a handcar house and stole some tools, helping them loosen a part of the track and tie it to a hidden rope. When the train came along, they pulled the rope, which jerked the rail out of place and caused the engine to plunge into the ditch, falling on its side. The engineer and fireman died, and several passengers were injured.

Jesse and Frank climbed into the express car and forced the guard to open the safe. Imagine their surprise when instead of the $75,000 worth of gold they were expecting, they found only $2,000 in currency. The gold shipment had been delayed. Their total take on this first moving train robbery: $3,000, which included the $2,000 in currency and other loot taken from the passengers.

News of the robbery soon spread around the nation. The outlaws had scattered and were sheltered by friends in Missouri. Later, the governor of Missouri offered a $10,000 reward for the capture of Jesse James, dead or alive. The reward proved to be too tempting for a newer member of Jesse's gang, as on April 3, 1882, Bob Ford shot and killed Jesse in his home in St. Joseph, Missouri.

This historic marker is on the site of the first train robbery in the West. Courtesy of Travel Iowa

Compute This!

John Vincent Atanasoff was seemingly a real-life "Young Sheldon," like the character from the TV show who was a genius from a young age. He figured out how to use his dad's slide rule at the age of nine, went through his mom's college algebra book for fun, and graduated from the University of Florida with a nearly perfect GPA in electrical engineering. Afterward he accepted a teaching position at Iowa State University.

During his time at ISU, he received a master's degree in math and a PhD in theoretical physics and taught, all the while thinking about ways to compute a series of problems more quickly than could be done by hand. A long drive east of Ames on Highway 30 and a stop at a bar to contemplate his mathematical problem were the tickets to his breakthrough.

Back at ISU, he asked for funds to hire an assistant and build a prototype of his computer. He received a small grant and hired Clifford Berry, a brilliant young graduate student. Over the next months, the two worked together to create a crude device that worked well enough to prove Atanasoff's theories correct. Atansoff named the device the ABC, the Atanasoff-Berry Computer.

Both men were called into military support services as World War II began, and neither had ensured their invention had a patent. Now there was a new problem. A fellow scientist, Johan Mauchly, a physicist at Ursinus College (north of Philadelphia), had been Atanasoff's houseguest. During his stay, Atanasoff had showed him detailed drawings, plans, and a working model of his computer.

You guessed it: Mauchly took the information and prepared his own version of the ABC and made a deal with the US Army to build his "Electronic Numerical Integrator and Computer" (ENIAC) for use in computing ballistics trajectories. Since this was considered top-

John Vincent Atanasoff stands in front of Iowa State University's Atanasoff Hall, which was named in his honor in 1988. Courtesy of Iowa State University Library Special Collections and University Archives

secret information, Atanasoff couldn't gain access to the device or to Mauchly's patents, which of course Mauchly had remembered to file.

Years later Mauchly had become known as the Father of the Computer, and other large companies contested the patents. A seven-year trial ensued, and ultimately the judge found that Mauchly's ENIAC was derived from Atanasoff's ABC, and Atanasoff emerged the winner.

Although Atanasoff never made any money off of his invention, he regained rightful credit as the developer of the world's first digital computer.

First Airline Stewardess in the US

Some people are lucky enough to know what they want to do from an early age. Ellen Church of Cresco was one of them. Born in 1904, one year after the Wright Brothers' famous flight, Church loved to watch airplanes at the county fair. She knew that someday she would learn to fly.

After graduating from Cresco High School, Church went into nursing. In her free time, she took flying lessons and earned her private pilot's license. Since she walked to work daily past the Boeing Air Transport office, she stopped in one day to ask for a job. The airline hired only male pilots, but she learned the company was planning to hire stewards, and Church knew she'd be great in that position. She was hired on a three-month trial basis on one stipulation: she could be head stewardess if she found seven other nurses to work on planes with her.

Besides the requirement that these seven others should be trained nurses, Boeing had other rigid qualifications: the nurses could weigh no more than 115 pounds, be no taller than 5'4", and had to be single women under the age of 25. They also had to be able to undertake rigorous job duties such as caring for sick and frightened passengers, loading and unloading luggage, helping fuel the plane, passing out lunches, cleaning inside the plane, and tightening the bolts that held the seats to the floor. It was much more taxing than simply taking tickets. These "Sky Girls," as Boeing called them, earned $125 per month for 100 hours of flying.

Church and her seven nurses proved they could do the job exceptionally well. However, after only 18 months she was forced to quit flying because of an auto accident injury. Church's career in the air went on as she joined the Army Nurse Corps during World War II, helping evacuate wounded soldiers from Africa and Italy by airplane.

Because of her unique background, Captain Ellen Church was called to train evacuation nurses for the D-Day invasion of France in 1944. She received several honors, including the Victory Medal for her "meritorious achievement in aerial flight." Church created a career out of flying at a time when many men did not take the idea of a woman working on a plane seriously.

Not bad for an Iowa girl who wanted to learn to fly.

Ellen Church and her Sky Girls, all professional nurses, under 25 years of age and unmarried . . . strict requirements of the time. Courtesy of Wikimedia Commons

I Taught Amelia Earhart to Fly!

Here's a woman of many "firsts": first female aviator in Iowa, first to run her own aviation business, and first female to run a commercial airfield.

Mary Anita "Neta" Snook Southern of Ames, or "Snooky," as her friends called her, was interested in machinery at an early age and followed this interest to Iowa State College (now University), where she took courses in mechanical drawing, engines, and farm machinery repair.

She became fascinated with aviation, applying to the Curtiss-Wright Aviation School in Newport News, Virginia, where she was denied admittance because no women were allowed. Instead, she became one of the first female student pilots in the Davenport Flying School in Iowa, which unfortunately closed after a major crash. Snooky eventually gained entry into Curtiss-Wright, the very school where she was once denied.

Neta Snook Southern ready for a flight at Kinner Field in 1921. Courtesy of Ames History Museum, Karsten Smedal private collection

She put in many hours in the air until civilian flights were banned during World War I. She then used her time testing aircraft parts and engines on their way to combat in Europe. She also bought a wrecked plane and spent two years rebuilding it. In 1920, she soloed in her rebuilt plane and received her pilot's license.

Snooky flew around the Midwest and made a living hauling sightseers even though her license didn't allow it. She charged $15 for a 15-minute plane ride.

She soon received her official license as a qualified pilot . . . and then the Midwest winters hit. Snooky headed to California, where she could fly year-round. She worked as an instructor at a new airport, Kinner Field, where her background in mechanical work made her invaluable to the business. Snooky soon became the first woman to run a commercial airfield.

In 1921, Amelia Earhart and her parents were looking for a female pilot for an instructor. Snooky taught Amelia to fly for $1 in Liberty bonds per minute in the air, but after the two became friends, the price dropped and Snooky volunteered her time. Initially, Snooky's student wasn't the best pilot, but practice made perfect, and the two women flew together for a year.

Snooky was married the following year to Bill Southern, got pregnant, and gave up flying. After Earhart disappeared in her famous flight in 1937, Snooky started speaking about her own career in aviation and wrote her autobiography, *I Taught Amelia to Fly*.

In 1981, Snooky was acknowledged as the oldest female pilot in the United States and died 10 years later at the age of 95. One year after her death, Neta Snook Southern was inducted into the Iowa Aviation Hall of Fame.

Champion of Women's Right to Vote

Carrie Chapman Catt, ready to speak at Continental Hall. Courtesy of Library of Congress

Carrie Chapman Catt took one word out of the US Constitution . . . and that word was "male." Growing up on a farm near Charles City, Carrie was full of curiosity. At 13, she asked her father why he voted and her mother didn't. She noticed that both her father and the hired man were dressed to go into town to vote while her mother wasn't. Her sincere question was greeted with laughter from her whole family. Voting, she was told, was simply too important a civic duty to leave to women. For Carrie, this was a defining moment and a turning point in her life.

Carrie set out to prove many things, one of the most important being that women were "smart enough to vote as well." She began with the foundation of a strong education. Carrie received a teaching certificate after finishing high school and taught in the summer months. After her first year of teaching, she enrolled at Iowa State University, the only woman in her class and later the valedictorian. She became superintendent of schools in Mason City and took charge on her first day, visiting schools where troublemakers disrupted class. With her two-foot strap of harness leather, she took disruptive students out of class and "impressed upon them who was boss."

Soon after meeting a talented journalist, Leo Chapman, she married him and assisted at the local newspaper, writing a column titled "Women's World." During this time, the Iowa legislature was considering a bill for municipal suffrage of women. Carrie gathered a petition with signatures

Carrie Chapman Catt's childhood home in Charles City.

of nearly every woman in town—the same technique she used when operating on the national stage.

She and Leo later moved to San Francisco, where Leo contracted typhoid fever and died. After moving back to Iowa, Carrie renewed a friendship with George Catt, and soon they married. Carrie founded the Iowa Woman Suffrage Association, organized the National American Woman Suffrage Association, and was handed the national presidency of this group by Susan B. Anthony.

In 1920, with the final ratification of the 19th Amendment, Carrie didn't stop for a second. She immediately organized the League of Women Voters to teach women how to use their vote. It's a good thing she was not only a compelling speaker with the power to inspire others, but also a person who understood the importance of education . . . and agitation.

Get into Align(ment)

Daniel David (D. D.) Palmer never had a problem earning a living. He once raised bees and carted gallons of honey to East Coast markets, pocketing thousands of dollars in profit. He also read every book he could find, especially if it was about the body and healing.

His search for knowledge led him to curing people by magnetic healing, and after he learned this art, he opened his own office in the mid-1880s, soon attracting a large clientele. While working as a magnetic healer, he became interested in finding the cause of all disease. This led him to the foundation of chiropractic. Palmer's theories revolved around the concept that altered nerve flow was indeed the cause of all disease, and misaligned spinal vertebrae affected nerve flow. He thought that restoring health would involve one thing: restoring vertebrae to their perfect alignment.

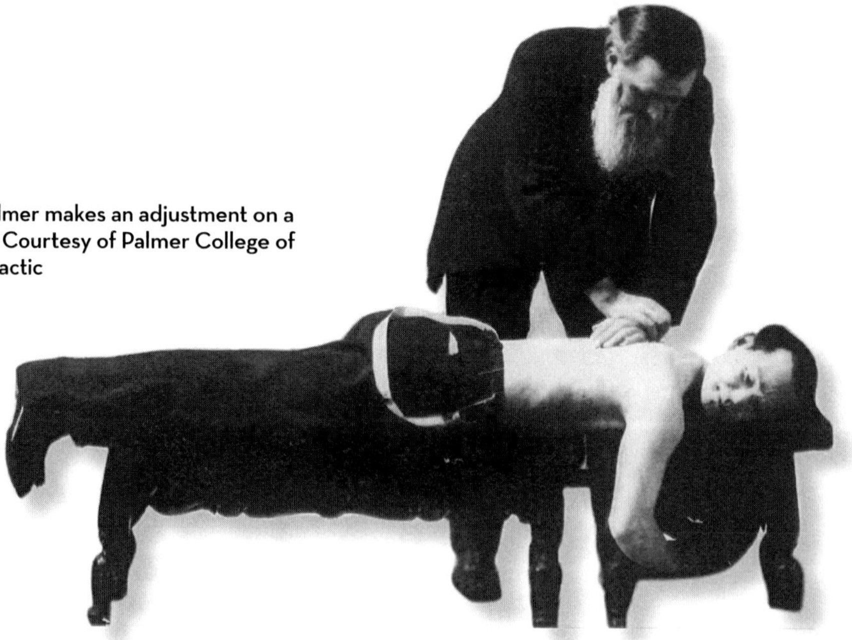

D. D. Palmer makes an adjustment on a patient. Courtesy of Palmer College of Chiropractic

An accidental "cure" of treating his janitor's deafness by righting his vertebrae caused Palmer to go back to his anatomy books in search of more answers. He practiced what he had discovered about pinched nerves being corrected by repositioning vertebrae, and early patients often left his office bruised and bleeding from his manipulations.

Palmer went on to found the Palmer School of Chiropractic, and after he was charged by the medical community with practicing medicine without a license, his son, B. J., bought his father out of the business. B. J.—and not his father—then became known as the developer of chiropractic. Under the leadership of B. J. and his wife, Mabel Heath, chiropractic rose to become the second-largest health care discipline.

D. D. and his son never reunited, and although his son took chiropractic to greater heights, D. D. will always be known as its founder.

One Society for All

Since D. D. Palmer gave the first recorded chiropractic treatment in 1895, four schools of chiropractic have begun in Iowa. Besides the Palmer College of Chiropractic, the National University of Health Sciences, Universal College of Chiropractic, and American School of Chiropractic began here. For years, two professional societies represented chiropractic physicians in Iowa. However, in 1964, the newly formed Iowa Chiropractic Society blended the two together in order for all Iowa chiropractors to have one unified voice.

Best Thing Since Sliced Bread

The saying, "It's the greatest thing since sliced bread" is a tribute to Otto Frederick Rohwedder of Davenport. A jeweler by trade, Rohwedder was interested in tinkering around with things. His love for finding ways to improve the machines he used in his jewelry business extended beyond his job, and eventually led him to the concept of a bread-slicing machine.

His determination to make sliced bread a reality was realized when the first automatically sliced commercial loaves were produced on July 6, 1928, in Chillicothe, Missouri, using the machine he invented. However, it wasn't smooth sailing getting to that point. He had a prototype and blueprints destroyed in a fire in 1917, and he also faced skepticism from bakers all over who told him factory-sliced bread would go stale quickly. After the fire, he had to raise funds and re-create the machinery. He also worked on a companion device to solve

One of the first brands to distribute sliced bread was Wonder Bread. Courtesy of Wikimedia Commons

the problem of sliced bread becoming stale more quickly, so his device was designed to slice and wrap the bread in one process.

He forged ahead and put his bread slicer into service at his friend Frank Bench's Chillicothe Baking Company. An enthusiastic report followed, with comments about the neat and precise slices that were better than someone could slice by hand with a bread knife.

Some bakers grumbled that automatically sliced bread was just a fad, but by 1930 it could be found in most towns around the country. One of the first brands to distribute sliced bread in that same year was Wonder, and Wonder Bread's popularity soared once it was marketed in sliced form.

Around the same time, the toaster was invented in Britain and was catching on fast in America. Using sliced bread was much easier and worked exceptionally well in this newfangled invention. Things were going well for Otto. Sliced bread was in demand!

And along came World War II. The War Rationing Board decided to ration sliced bread to reduce consumption of the waxed paper in which sliced loaves were wrapped. Because steel was also rationed, the government didn't want any more bread-slicing machines to be made. There was so much public outcry that the government rescinded the ban.

Fast-forward to today, and as much as 80 percent of bread is sliced. Thank you, Otto!

Home of the American Cream Draft Horse

The *only* draft horse native to the United States originated in three towns: Jewell, Ellsworth, and Radcliffe. The American Cream horse was developed during the first half of the 20th century and is characterized by the cream or gold champagne color of its coat. This horse has a unique history unlike that of any other draft breed.

Time to show off American Cream draft horses, developed in Iowa. Courtesy of Wikimedia Commons

Its journey began in the early 1900s with Old Granny, a mare whose cream-colored coat, pink skin, and amber-colored eyes set her apart. The breed is known for its exceptional beauty and gentle spirit. American Creams are much more than a pretty face, however. They possess a calm and willing nature that makes them ideal partners for individuals new to draft horses, fostering a sense of trust and companionship.

The average weight of mares can be up to 1,800 pounds, and stallions can reach 2,000 pounds. These draft horses have ample draft hindquarters; a well-muscled chest; short, strong legs; and are well-proportioned. American Cream horses range in height from 15 to 16.3 hands. This breed has a good disposition and is uniform in color and type, making for an easily matched team.

Old Granny's legacy lived on through her offspring, and these gentle giants were so highly appreciated that in 1944 the American Cream Horse Association of America was established. Five years later, the Iowa Department of Agriculture granted this breed the same status as other established draft breeds and solidified its place in American agriculture.

An exceptionally rare breed, the American Cream horse is critically endangered, with only approximately 400 remaining worldwide. And why is this? It's simply because farm tractors replaced draft animals, thus making the demand for draft horses plummet.

In 1982, dedicated breeders came together to breathe new life into the association, reigniting the passion for preserving this rare breed. Hopefully, these magnificent creatures will continue to delight future generations with their gentle temperaments, impressive stature, and incredible beauty.

Pony of the Americas Club Born in Iowa

A Shetland pony breeder (and lawyer) from Mason City, Les Boomhower got the idea to set up a new breed registry when he bought a foal bred from a Shetland stallion and an Arabian/Appaloosa mare. Strict guidelines were set to be registered as POA, and the breed was designed for children to ride and show. From this original POA, a world championship show was born. Perfect for trail and endurance riding, ranch work and hunting, the POA is gentle, durable and intelligent. Another first for Iowa's equine fans!

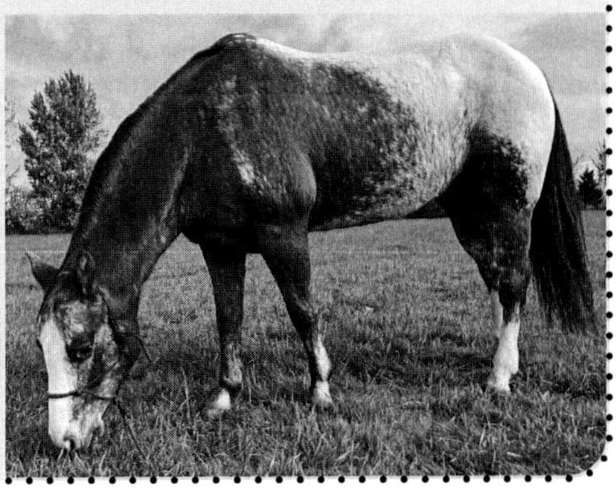

Pony of the Americas. Courtesy of Wikimedia Commons

A sculpture titled *Estherville Meteorite* sits in Estherville's Liberty Square. Courtesy of Estherville Chamber of Commerce

It's a Bird! It's a Plane! It's a . . . Meteorite!

Imagine going about your business when the earth starts to tremble and china shifts on your cupboard shelves while your doors and windows rattle. You hear a terrific explosion followed by thunderous sounds, and some of your windows begin to shatter. You look to the sky and see what appears to be a large ball of fire. Maybe this wouldn't shake the nerves of someone in an earthquake-prone area like California, but in Iowa, it would certainly cause some great alarm!

This is what happened on the afternoon of May 10, 1879, when a 455-pound meteorite fell to earth in Emmet County just a few miles north of Estherville. It was the largest meteorite known to have fallen in North America and has now become known as the Estherville Meteorite.

It was on that late Saturday afternoon in 1879 when the explosion (followed by thunderous sounds) was heard around town, and a large body of fire traveled in the sky from the southwest to the northeast.

A meteor had fallen! The main body of the mass broke apart into pieces as it descended. Two people found themselves directly under the mass when it exploded and reported that the three large pieces went in different directions, trailing ribbons of vapor. Three people north of town (more than half a mile apart) saw dirt fly high into the air. A herd boy near Superior said that falling stones had caused his cattle to stampede. Some boys at Four Mile Lake said the calm water had been peppered with small pebbles.

Estherville had never seen anything like this in its history. Later, three large meteor pieces were found weighing 431, 151, and 106 pounds, along with several smaller specimens. When the largest mass struck, it buried itself 15 feet into the ground. Portions of the meteorite can be viewed on display in the Smithsonian Museum of Natural History, the Estherville Public Library, and the Naturhistorisches Museum in Vienna, Austria. A piece of the meteorite was purchased in 2010 and now resides in the Meteorite Center in Estherville.

What's So Great about a Meteorite?

Did you know that over 48 tons of meteoritic material falls on Earth each day? Scientists do, and they also say that several meteors per hour can usually be seen on a clear night. NASA also tells us that most meteorites are between the size of a pebble and a fist, and less than 5% of the original object usually makes it to the ground. Imagine just how large the Estherville Meteorite was before it hit Earth's atmosphere!

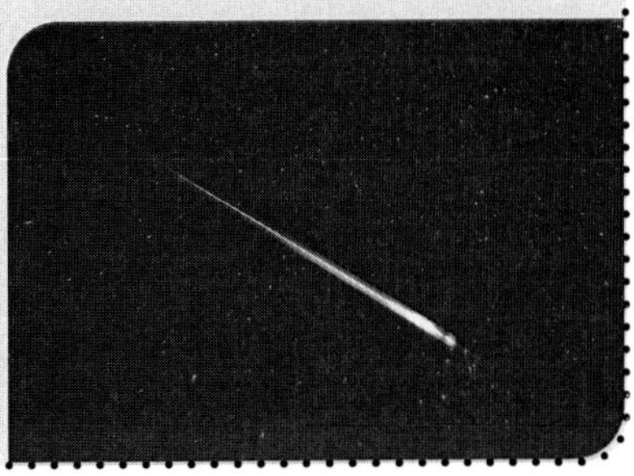

There is more to a meteorite than meets the eye. Courtesy of Wikimedia Commons

Tractor Power

John Froelich's problem was getting farmers to keep their horses in the barn and use the many "horses" in his gasoline-powered tractor instead. A grain elevator operator in Froelich (a small town in Clayton County named for his father), John bought a gasoline engine in 1890 to power his elevator. Once it was installed, he took one of the new engines and put it on a steam engine base.

Townspeople made fun of his tractor (the name derived from his TRACtion moTOR) but cheered him on when they saw the tractor moving at an impressive speed of 3 miles an hour, which was "roughly the pace of a brisk stroll." Watching the machine move, especially to people who had never witnessed anything like it, was unforgettable.

John further tested his tractor on a neighbor's farm and then loaded it on a train to South Dakota and used it to thresh over a thousand bushels of wheat a day, using only 26 gallons of gas. John found others to invest in a company that would build and sell tractors, and they called it the Waterloo Gasoline Traction Engine Company, making John the president. Out of the four tractors this company built, two were sold and both were returned.

Times were tough not only for the company but also for the nation in the 1890s. The company decided to build only stationary gas engines to provide income. It was at this point that John wanted out. His main interest was in tractors—the kind that could be driven backward and forward—and not just the stationary engines that the company was now focused on. The group sold one of its stationary engines to the *Waterloo Courier* newspaper pressroom and then sold out to another group who formed the Waterloo Gasoline Engine Company.

John lost most of his savings and property during this period and sold his interest in the company, moving to Dubuque and working for a company that manufactured gasoline engines. Meanwhile, the Waterloo Gasoline Engine Company improved its tractor and stationary engines and attracted the attention of John Deere and Company. Deere made an offer and acquired the Waterloo plant.

John Froelich and his gasoline-powered tractor "transformed the prairie sod and changed world food production as no other invention had done." He will always be remembered for his contribution to agriculture, and the town bearing his name, Froelich, Iowa, "Tractor Town USA."

Invented by John Froelich in 1892, this gasoline-powered tractor paved the way for others. Courtesy of Froelich Foundation for the Preservation of Farm Tractor History (froelichtractor.com)

Ease the Pain

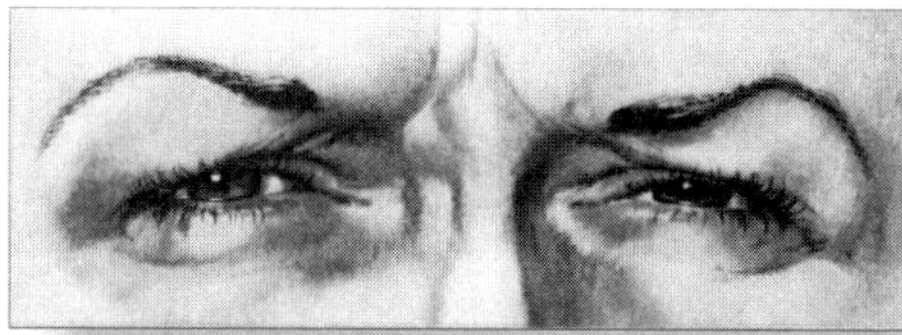

Bufferin eased the pain of a headache without upsetting the stomach. Courtesy of Wikimedia Commons

What do you do when you're in pain and need quick relief? Before the days of Tylenol and other acetaminophen products, people reached for their aspirin. However, this "wonder drug" was a double-edged sword. In curing people of their aches and pains, simple aspirin often caused a stomachache as well. Enter the team physician for the University of Iowa athletes, William D. "Shorty" Paul, MD, and his colleague, Joseph Routh, PhD.

"Shorty" treated many patients with daily doses of aspirin to ease pain; however, he couldn't help those whose stomachs couldn't handle the harsh acidity of the medication. One day, Shorty used an antacid he had received to use in experiments in conjunction with the aspirin in treating a colleague complaining of a headache. Dietitian Kate Daum, head of the Department of Nutrition at the University of Iowa, had initially declined the aspirin Shorty offered her because it tended to upset her stomach. But when the aspirin was "buffered" by the antacid, she reported that her headache left and her calm stomach remained.

Creating large quantities of the combined product proved troublesome because of its short shelf life. Shorty contacted Joseph Routh, who studied the buffer's properties and its interactions with aspirin. Together, they concocted a successful formula. After a two-year study at the University of Iowa, Bristol-Myers learned of the remedy; soon afterward, the product, Bufferin, popped up in pharmacies all over the world.

Shorty and Joseph then developed an over-the-counter stomach antacid version of the product, which came to be known as Rolaids. Since the two doctors never applied for a patent, they never received any royalties from either Bufferin or Rolaids. Their contribution to pain relief, however, is quite an accomplishment indeed.

Who Was Kate Daum?

A nutritionist at the University of Iowa, Daum was Dr. Paul's colleague who had a headache but couldn't stomach aspirin. Besides trying his "buffered aspirin" and finding that it worked for her, Daum did many notable studies of her own, including dietetics in the hospital field and research on the effects of skipping breakfast. Signs of fatigue, slower reaction times, a bad attitude, and lower scholastic abilities should be some evidence of the importance of eating before heading out in the morning.

Courtesy of Wikimedia Commons

Ice Cream Capital of the World

Blue Bunny makes more ice cream than "any other place in the world," and rightly so; they have the largest freezer of its kind in North America, and it reaches 12 stories high!

Back in 1913, Fred H. Wells Jr. paid $250 to a local dairy farmer in Le Mars, Iowa, for a horse, a delivery wagon, a few cans and jars, and the goodwill of the milk business. What did this get him? A milk distribution route and a guaranteed source of milk from a herd of just 15 cows. Fred delivered milk around town, house to house, seven days a week in his horse-drawn wagon.

Fred partnered with his brother, Harry C. Wells, to start the Wells Ice Cream Company of Sioux City in 1925. It soon became a hit, and the Wells brothers sold the company to a competitor, Fairmont Creamery, in 1929. This sale helped the family stay afloat during the Depression years.

Never ones to give up on their dreams, the brothers wanted to get back into the ice cream business in 1935, but they needed a new name. The new company name was born when Fred and Harry held a "Name That Ice Cream" contest with a cash prize of $25. A man from Sioux City, Iowa, submitted "Blue Bunny" because he noticed how his young son enjoyed the blue bunnies in a department store's window around Easter. Not only did John VandenBrink win the contest, but the name has stuck to this day.

Many years later, in 1994, Le Mars was named the "Ice Cream Capital of the World." By 2019, the Wells Visitor Center and Ice Cream Parlor served over 200,000 visitors annually. One thing, however, remains the same: a great family history that began with a single delivery wagon and grew into the world's largest family-owned and managed ice cream producer. What a sweet story!

Ice Cream Is Always in Style

Wells Blue Bunny is in good company for ice cream lovers in Iowa. Two other iconic ice cream parlors that opened near the turn of the century are Wilton's Candy Kitchen (Wilton), established in 1860 as a confectionery adding ice cream later, and Birdsall's Ice Cream (Mason City), established in 1931. Step back into time and experience ice cream the old-fashioned way with some of the original recipes and ever-changing new flavors that keep customers coming back for more.

Wells Visitor Center and Ice Cream Parlor makes thousands of people happy annually. Courtesy of Travel Iowa

Birthplace of the Greatest Show on Earth

"Iowa is probably one of the mothers of the circus," touts Peter Wagner, a past president of the Circus Fans Association of America. During the years between immigrating from Germany and living in Wisconsin, the seven Ringling brothers and their parents spent a dozen years in McGregor, Iowa.

The origin of "The Greatest Show on Earth" goes back to the spring of 1870 when Dan Rice's Great Paris Pavilion Circus (a riverboat show) docked in McGregor. The Ringling sons were there to watch, and they were absolutely enthralled by what they saw. The one thing on their minds when they returned home was planning and rehearsing their own backyard show. The brothers put on their first show in a hayloft in McGregor, charging an admittance "fee" of straight pins used in women's hair, which at the time were quite a commodity.

The following year, the Ringling brothers added a tent to their show; it was made from the discarded canvas cover of a covered wagon on its way west. A street parade was called for, complete with a toy wagon, fife, and drum. And still this show cost only 10 straight pins!

Always looking for something to add, next up was the acquisition of a goat, complete with a little harness. Admission jumped to a penny. An old mustang with a wagon, a jaw harp, an accordion, a trumpet, and a drum boosted the admission to 5 cents. And then came

The Ringling Brothers and their family circa 1890. Courtesy of Wikimedia Commons

the tricks. Al spun a hat and some china on a pole; Otto drove the goat, and John was the clown. The brothers even did some trick riding on the old horse, and all of the brothers performed on the hoops and trapeze.

From their inaugural show, the brothers kept at it, struggling for a few years to put on their shows. Through thick and thin, though, the show was the thing. The Ringling family eventually moved across the river to Prairie du Chien, Wisconsin, and they launched their full-fledged circus when they were settled in Baraboo, Wisconsin, which later became home to the Circus World Museum. And the rest is history.

The Show Must Go On

In 1880, the Ringling Brothers circus was set to perform in Onslow, Iowa. A big storm blew through town, ripping their circus tent to shreds, ruining much of their equipment, and forcing them to cancel their show.

With no money from the show, they couldn't repay what they had borrowed to purchase their animals' food, so the shop owners kept some of their animals until payment could be made.

The brothers trudged 15 miles through mud to Monticello, where they hoped doing one show would get them back on track financially. No such luck. However, in Cascade, almost every person in town pitched in to help the Ringling Brothers in their time of need.

The performances went better than expected, with enough money to pay their bills and then some. From that point on, the Ringling Brothers Circus prospered.

And for the rest of the circus's history, the people of Cascade were always remembered. Al Ringling said, "Anyone from Cascade is free to this show anytime!"

First Fast Food Franchise . . . "Made Right!"

Fred Angell owned a Muscatine butcher shop that he wished were a restaurant. He experimented with the right combination of a special cut and grind of meat and a selected blend of spices, and ended up inventing a new sandwich in the process. It was definitely not a hamburger, but more of a "loose meat" sandwich that could be compared to a sloppy joe without the tomato-based sauce. He served one steaming hot to a delivery man who happened to drop by the shop one morning. The delivery man's delight in the sandwich was evident. "Fred, you know this sandwich is made right!" he exclaimed. The Maid-Rite was born on the spot.

What's in a Maid-Rite? One hundred percent low-fat, lean beef with no filler that is trimmed to stringent specifications and steamed in the unique Maid-Rite cooker, along with special seasoning. Of course, a spoon comes with the sandwich to pick up the spillover. A warm bun, mustard, pickle, and onions finish out the Maid-Rite, all Iowan and made right!

In 1926, Fred established America's first fast-food franchises. He sold franchisee rights in Newton in 1927 and Marshalltown in 1928. Franchise rights included the brand name and secret formula for menu items. Buildings were required to have the same design, with a white exterior and red stripes.

All of this required much hard work and determination on Fred's part. In the early days, he butchered and ground his meat in his own basement. He also made the ice cream from scratch and mixed the private label root beer.

Step back into time in Muscatine's first Maid-Rite.

The hard work paid off as the franchises took off. Many of the original franchises granted in the 1920s are still in operation. Not only that, but families found a place within this Maid-Rite franchise, with third-generation family members often operating these iconic restaurants.

As if the sandwiches and franchises weren't enough, later Fred established another first: drive-up and walk-up windows for customers' convenience. Thanks to his innovative ideas, people in Muscatine and beyond have enjoyed the lasting and delicious tradition he started with a little experimentation and a lot of hard work.

He Made 'Em Scream for "I-Scream!"

A young college man was riding a train home to Onawa and happened to notice a huge tub of ice cream being hoisted onto the train. Christian K. Nelson arrived at home and asked his father to go into the ice cream business. He must have been very convincing, because the next year, the Nelson Creamery sold 10,000 gallons of ice cream.

Eskimo Pie inventor Christian Kent Nelson in 1922. Courtesy of Wikimedia Commons

After Nelson graduated from college, he returned to his hometown to teach and to open his own ice cream store. The year was 1921, and his life was about to change, all because an 8-year-old boy couldn't decide between ordering a chocolate bar or a scoop of ice cream.

The little boy agonized over his important decision and finally ordered a candy bar—which Nelson happened to be out of. The boy then ordered an ice cream sandwich, but as Nelson was making it, the boy changed his mind to ask for a different brand of candy bar. Nelson asked him why he didn't just buy *both*, and the boy replied, "Sure, I know—I want 'em both, but I only got a nickel!"

This dilemma helped Nelson come up with the revolutionary idea to combine both . . . an ice cream bar on a stick and coated with chocolate. If only he could figure out a way for something hot to stick to something frozen. Experiment after experiment produced failure after failure, until a chocolate salesman mentioned that the "chocolate used in candy held more cocoa butter than cocoa." Nelson increased the cocoa butter proportion, and the frozen bar and hot chocolate became one.

Nelson secured a patent for his "I-Scream bar," but didn't have a lot of luck selling it to a manufacturer. However, it captured the interest of Russell Stover, the candy confectioner, who took one look at the ice cream bar, quit his job, and negotiated a deal with Nelson. The partners changed the name of the frozen treat to the Eskimo Pie, secured a patent, and started the Eskimo Pie Corporation.

The pies wrapped in aluminum foil sold extremely well in Des Moines and Chicago, and within four months the partners had sold 2,700 franchises. By the following spring, sales averaged one million Eskimo Pies daily. Within 19 months, one billion pies had been sold. Nelson was able to retire at the age of 35, and it was all due to an indecisive young boy.

Eskimo Pies are now Edy's Pies. Same product . . . different name. Courtesy of Freepik

A (Delicious) Apple a Day

Jesse Hiatt had a lot of responsibility at a young age. At 17, he took over the family farm in Pennsylvania to support his parents. After they died, he moved to Madison County in Iowa and bought some land near his brother's place. He planted an orchard in honor of the one he had left behind and with his brother hauled a wagonload of trees from Oskaloosa, which was 77 miles away.

When he noticed a little shoot that had sprung out of the root of a Bellflower apple seedling that had died, he let it grow. Not only did the shoot blossom, but it grew into a beautiful apple tree and produced fruit like Hiatt had never seen. The apple was elongated, streaked with red and yellow, and had a wonderful aroma and incredibly good taste. Hiatt named it "Hawkeye" in honor of his newly adopted state of Iowa. Over the next 11 years, he traveled and told others about the superior

These Delicious apples are thanks to Jesse Hiatt, who discovered them in the 1870s. Courtesy of Wikimedia Commons

Hawkeye apple, but there was very little interest, especially with other farmers who would have to grow them for themselves.

Around this same time, there was a contest to find the best apple in the world. Hiatt entered his apples, and they were declared the best apples ever seen or tasted! However, there was a small problem: Hiatt couldn't find his contest entry card, so he wasn't able to be declared the winner.

Fortunately, the contest was offered again the following year. Entering the contest once more, Hiatt didn't realize he had already won the prize. Clarence Stark of Stark Brothers Nursery traveled to Peru, Iowa, and bought the exclusive right to propagate and disseminate the Hawkeye apple. Stark decided that the name wouldn't sell and changed it to "Delicious."

The Delicious tree seemed to be almost perfect, not requiring much pruning or shaping, and it always grew to have hardy branches that bent with the weight of the fruit, but didn't break. From Jesse Hiatt's one original apple tree, over fifteen million apple trees have been produced. And over 60 percent of all apple trees in the world today have come from this single Iowa apple tree, producing offshoots of the original Delicious apple, the Red Delicious and Golden Delicious.

Jessie Field Shambaugh with roses in Page County between 1906 and 1912. Courtesy of Jessie Field Shambaugh Papers, Iowa Women's Archives, University of Iowa Libraries

The Mother of 4-H

A proud farm girl from the start, Jessie Field asked a lot of questions, and her father answered them. In doing so, Jessie learned to be as proud of her farm heritage as her father was.

She graduated from Shenandoah High School, attended Western Normal College in Shenandoah, and during the middle of her sophomore year was asked to fill a teaching vacancy in a small country school in Clarinda. At first, she was thrilled to teach other farm children like she had been . . . until she discovered neither the boys nor the girls knew the basics. She formed a Boys' Corn Club to teach the boys successful farming basics and a Girls' Home Club to teach the girls more domestic duties. Jessie stressed learning by doing so the students could see the results of their work and develop pride in their accomplishments. Both students and parents were enthusiastic about these clubs and what they taught.

Soon, Jessie returned to college for her bachelor's degree. Following that, she became a principal in Montana and was then asked to return to Iowa to become a superintendent of 130 country schools. She bought a horse and buggy so she could visit each school three times a year. Her salary for such an important job? A whopping $33.50 a month!

"Miss Jessie" inspired her teachers to form Boys' and Girls' Clubs and brought in professors from Iowa State University to teach short courses for them. The program not only went well, but her students earned prizes in things like baking, sewing, and corn and livestock judging.

She continued to provide new opportunities for students such as agriculture competitions that included soil testing and corn judging to help motivate the children. She also organized countywide junior achievement shows, which were somewhat similar to today's fairs. The first Junior Exhibit was held in the fall of 1906 at the Farmers Institute in the basement of the Clarinda Armory.

As a tangible reward for the students, she designed a three-leaf clover pin with the letter "H" which stood for Head, Heart, and Hands. The next year, she added another H for Home (later changing to Health). Thus began the 4-H program, all thanks to a curious little farm girl.

The Corn Lady

As county superintendent of schools in Page County, Jessie Field wrote a book about her early days as a country school teacher. Entitled *The Corn Lady: The Story of a Country Teacher's Work*, this book (published in 1911) was written as a series of letters to her father. A farm girl through and through, Jessie was thrilled to share her love of agriculture and home economics with her students. She "loved the land and the people who raised the corn" and appreciated the moniker of "The Corn Lady," which was given to her by the people in her new town. It said to her, "You are one of us."

Keep Poppin'

A weekend tradition in our family included sharing popcorn and watching TV together. Dad popped it the good old-fashioned way on the stove, and each one of us got our own bowl full of buttery, salty goodness. Tradition also ran in the family business of creating the first official brand of popcorn, which was started right here in Iowa. Jolly Time Popcorn (or in its early days, the American Pop Corn Company) originated in 1914 by Cloid Smith and his son, Howard. Today, the Jolly Time Popcorn company is still family owned and operated by their descendants.

Cloid Smith started the first popcorn company, the "Official Snack of Happiness." Courtesy of Jolly Time Popcorn Company

How did they get into the popcorn business in the first place? The story is that Cloid bought farmland in Sac County in the summer of 1914 and got into an argument over the price of his grain in the fall. He was challenged to find another market for it, so he hauled it to Sioux City in his horse and buggy, and he and his son hand-shelled their first crop of popcorn in their basement. A year later, the operation expanded to their garage, and a year after that to their present site on the outskirts of Sioux City.

This long history that led to Jolly Time Popcorn being known as the "Official Snack of Happiness" involved a lot of hard work, creativity, and innovation. Cloid and Howard shelled, cleaned, and packaged 75,000 pounds of popcorn in their first year, all by hand and in their basement. Not only did their company receive the *Good Housekeeping* seal of approval later in 1925, but Jolly Time also developed a metal can to store their popcorn for freshness.

First can of popcorn sold in grocery stores. Courtesy of Jolly Time Popcorn Company

Over the years, popcorn brought families together, even during the Depression. Popcorn was an affordable snack at home or at the movies, and its popularity continued to grow through the years. Jolly Time was on TV and endorsed by celebrities. The company remained innovative, introducing its first microwave popcorn in 1983. Since then, Jolly Time has rolled out flavors galore.

One thing remains constant: the love of popcorn. Ever evolving to answer customer needs, Jolly Time is still a family business and is run by the fourth generation of Smiths today. What's the secret of their longevity? "Make something great; share it with people, and keep poppin'!"

From First to Last One-of-a-Kind Hotel

The Historic Park Inn, the last remaining hotel in the world designed by Frank Lloyd Wright, sits overlooking Mason City's Central Park. Listed on the National Register of Historic Places, this one-of-a-kind hotel opened in the fall of 1910, became a retail establishment housing several offices, and then fell into disrepair over the next 50 years. Thanks to the preservation efforts of Wright on the Park, the Historic Park Inn sits fully restored and awaits visitors from around the world to stay in its 27 boutique-style rooms and eat/drink in its restaurant and lounge.

Architecture fans appreciate a visit here to revel in the style that only Wright could envision. Beginning in 1907, local attorneys J.E.E. Markley and James E. Blythe commissioned Wright to design a hotel and bank right in the heart of Mason City. Wright's original plan for the hotel was a unique space "blending his signature Prairie School architectural style with the latest in modern amenities, including indoor plumbing and electricity."

Of course, there was a glitch during the construction in 1909. It had nothing to do with the actual construction of the building itself, but everything to do with Wright and his personal "affairs." While the hotel was under construction, Wright abruptly left town to travel to Europe with Mamah Cheney, a woman with whom he was having an affair. This caused tension with the building owners, and Wright never returned to Mason City.

Despite the setback, the Park Inn Hotel and City National Bank were completed in 1910. A new favorite among travelers, it quickly gained popularity. Over the years, however, the building fell into disrepair and closed in 1972. What was once a treasure of the city now housed a few retail establishments and several offices.

In 2005, a group of local preservationists formed an organization called Wright on the Park and launched a multi-year campaign to bring the hotel back to its original glory. It was a massive undertaking, but the Historic Park Inn Hotel reopened in 2011.

HPI (as the town affectionately calls it) has become a destination not only for architecture and Frank Lloyd Wright fans, but also for history buffs and travelers who appreciate great accommodations, wedding couples who choose this spot to celebrate, and conference attendees who appreciate the ambience. This unique example of Wright's vision continues to delight people from all over the world.

An architectural gem, the Historic Park Inn in Mason City welcomes guests from all over the world. Courtesy of Visit Mason City

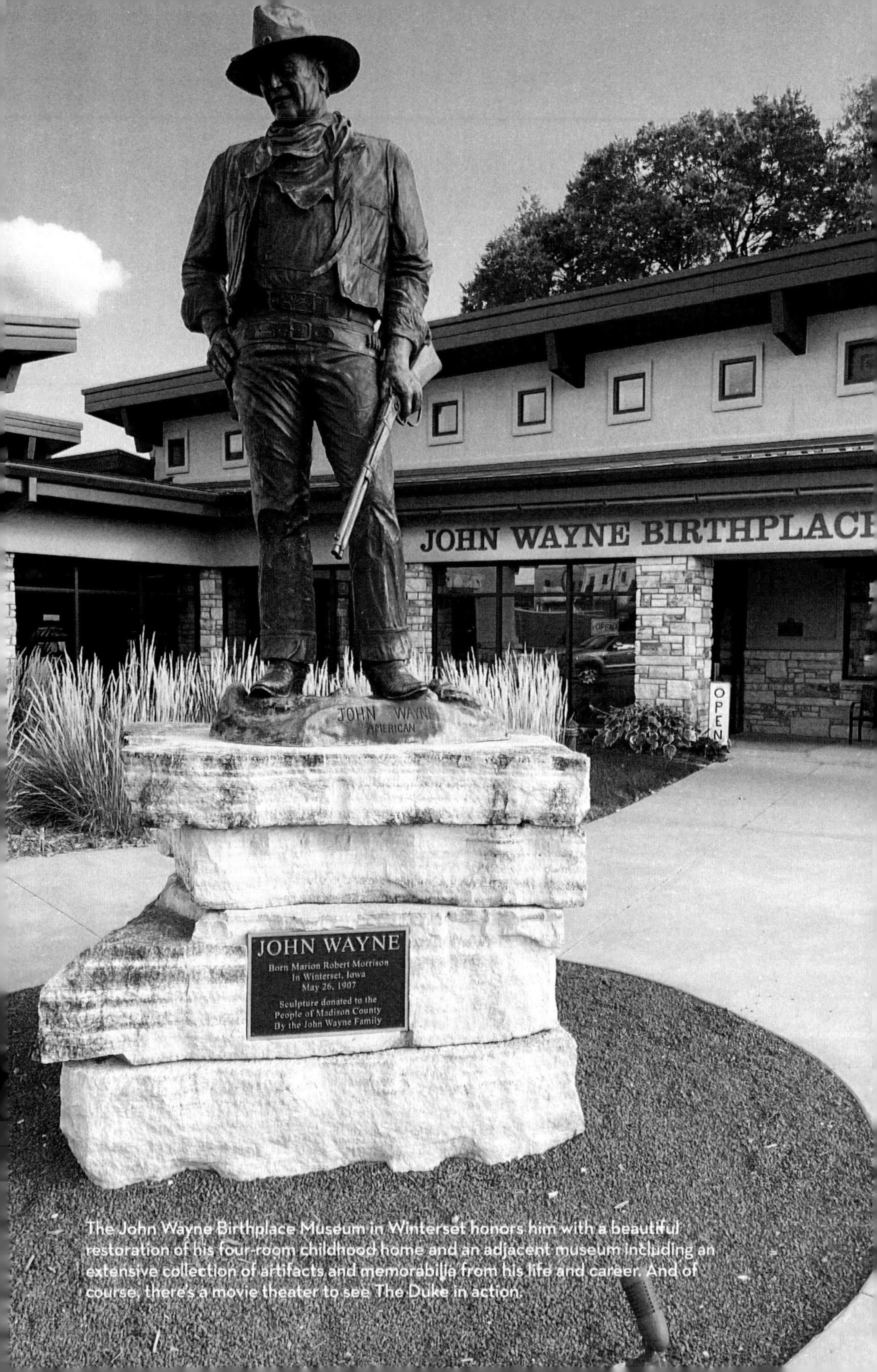

The John Wayne Birthplace Museum in Winterset honors him with a beautiful restoration of his four-room childhood home and an adjacent museum including an extensive collection of artifacts and memorabilia from his life and career. And of course, there's a movie theater to see The Duke in action.

Chapter Two

Famous Iowans

Sometimes fame doesn't always follow good deeds, a scintillating personality, or an exceptional talent. Sometimes it is quite the reverse. Iowa has produced many famous people; some were born here and some simply blossomed here.

Peruse the history books and you'll find tons of talent. Great singers, great writers, great cooks . . . Iowa has seen more than its fair share of amazingly talented people. However, one sister act in Iowa's history was so bad they became famous for it. In another case, a woman became famous for writing books she couldn't even tell people she had written.

Many a humanitarian has been recognized in this great state, but one held the top office in the country. And another put her life on the line to save others, way back in the days before easier ways to do so had been invented.

And sometimes, you just go on about your business, doing whatever it takes to get where you want to go, even if it involves using transportation of a very unique nature. It's in these times that others stop to take notice of the little things, the big things, and all those in between that can transform an ordinary person into a celebrity.

America's Painter Laureate

Grant Wood painted what he knew best—the landscapes and people of his home state. Courtesy of Library of Congress

Growing up on his family farm in Anamosa, Grant Wood painted what he knew. He loved watching his father hook up the team for plowing, and he ran into his kitchen to grab a charred stick from his mother so he could draw everything he observed on the farm on cardboard or wrapping paper. He drew his house, the barn, and the farm animals, having a special affinity for the chickens and roosters.

Grant was 10 years old when his father died. His mother sold the farm and moved the family to Cedar Rapids, where Grant continued to draw. Later, he worked at the Cedar Rapids Art Association, which had a gallery over the public library. It was there that Grant began to thoroughly study art books. He made some extra money by sleeping in the gallery, acting as a sort of amateur night watchman.

A unique thing about Grant's artistic talent was that he had an excellent visual memory, and he could describe a painting in great detail even years after seeing it. He was a self-taught artist, and his "school" was trial and error. He added to his skills by taking a few classes in Minneapolis and at the University of Iowa after he graduated from high school. After a stint in the Army, Grant returned home to Cedar Rapids and was hired to teach art in the public school system, despite having no training and only a small amount of experience as a teacher.

During an artist's trip to France where Grant tried to mimic French impressionism, things just weren't working out for him. He ran into an old friend from Cedar Rapids who was working in Paris, and the two of them got together for a long lunch to talk about life. Grant suddenly realized that he should go back to Iowa and paint what he knew best:

the "honest faces of people of the soil, the barns, hills, crops and things rural." The first person he saw when he returned to Iowa was his mother, and he saw her in a new and lovely light—so he painted her. His *Woman with Plants* is hailed by many critics as being among his finest work.

In 1930, another painting surpassed it. Grant achieved national fame with *American Gothic,* the often-parodied portrait of a stern-faced Iowa farmer and daughter. Grant's work simply spoke to people… then and now.

The Mysterious *American Gothic* Couple

When a picture of Wood's *American Gothic* was printed in newspapers, Iowa farm wives were in an uproar because they thought it was meant to caricature them.

The real story behind the painting was that Wood found a "trim white cottage with a trim white porch" on the farm that he liked. He chose his dentist and his own sister, Nan, to pose as severely strait-laced characters. He ordered the prim, colonial print apron and the trim, spotless overalls by mail from Chicago for his "models" and had his dentist hold a three-tined pitchfork in one hand. Just a man and his "daughter" enjoying their small-town life. . . .

When you live in Iowa and love theatre, there's a high probability you will appear onstage in *The Music Man* at least once in your life. And here is that one time for my parents, Wanda and Lyle Sprout of Charles City, who were ready to go onstage as the American Gothic couple in Mason City Community Theatre's production in 1996.

Spaced Out

Sometimes it's hard to dream big when you live right in the middle of the country on a hog and soybean farm. This was the case with Peggy Whitson, who grew up in Beaconsfield. At 9 years old, she looked to the sky when the Apollo 11 mission put men on the moon for the first time. Suddenly, that dream seemed possible.

Until the year of her high school graduation, however, it was unheard of for women to go into space flight. This was in 1978, when the first female astronauts were chosen. All of a sudden her dreams became goals. After graduating from Mt. Ayr High School, Whitson received her bachelor's degree in biology and chemistry from Iowa Wesleyan College and then her PhD from Rice University in Houston, Texas.

Just before Whitson graduated from Rice, her college advisors discouraged her from pursuing a career in space, urging her to go into medicine instead. They predicted that astronauts would be obsolete by the time she reached her goal. She forged ahead on the path she always knew she wanted to take.

That path wasn't without obstacles. She heard the word "No" too many times and worked hard for 10 years to get into NASA's astronaut training program. She worked on various research and development projects, held leadership roles, and worked with the US-USSR Joint Working Group in Space Medicine and Biology, giving her a broad range of valuable experience.

Finally, this Iowa girl was going to space! She spent six months on the International Space Station for her first expedition, nine months for her next, and nine months for her final mission with NASA. She is now considered America's most experienced astronaut (male or female),

Dreaming big led Peggy Whitson right where she wanted to be—in space! Courtesy of Axiom Space

spending over 665 days in space over five missions. In short, she holds the American record for the most time in space.

Breaking barriers didn't come easily for her, but her motivation and persistence paid off. Whitson was the first female and first non-military chief of the Astronaut Office. She retired from NASA in 2018 to join a private space infrastructure firm, Axiom Space, where she not only spent another 10 days in space, but also is helping engineer the space suits and stations of the future.

Peggy Whitson carved out her own path from the time she was a young girl. Taking advantage of every opportunity, learning along the way, and keeping her eyes on the sky were all crucial to helping Peggy achieve her dreams.

The World's Worst Sister Act

The Cherry Sisters were "celebrated" as being the world's worst sister act. Sometimes the "celebrations" involved getting pelted with rotten vegetables. Courtesy of Wikimedia Commons

The Cherry Sisters from Cedar Rapids had an act that was so bad, it was good. They decided to go onstage to boost their family fortune, staging, directing, and performing a show they had written themselves. *Something Good, Something Sad* contained a little bit of everything: patriotic ballads, bad poetry, interpretive dance, and one-act morality plays. The sisters—Addie, Jesse, Effie, and occasionally Lizzie—didn't let a little thing like a lack of talent get in their way.

Audiences found themselves rolling in the aisles with laughter, and they routinely "rewarded" the Cherry Sisters with rotten tomatoes, peach pits, cigar butts, and cabbages. In fact, so many things were thrown at them that it became necessary to have a screen of chicken wire between the stage and the seats for safety's sake.

Any other performer might have been disheartened by having projectiles thrown at them nightly. Not so with these sisters! Since a fair share of coins hit the stage along with the rotten vegetables, they assumed the audience was rewarding them for their efforts and the vegetables "came from a misguided minority that couldn't appreciate true art when they saw it."

The reputation of "The World's Worst Sister Act" assisted in packing vaudeville houses all over Iowa. By 1896, news of their act reached New York and the struggling Oscar Hammerstein, whose theater, the

How Would *You* Like *These* Reviews?

"They couldn't sing, speak or act. They were simply awful. . . . At one minute the scene was like the incurable ward in an insane asylum, the next it was like a camp meeting. Cigars, cigarettes, everything was thrown at them, yet they stood there awkwardly, bowing their acknowledgments, and singing on."—*Cedar Rapids Gazette*, March 1893

"They began as the four worst professional actresses in the world and ended without improving one iota."—*The American Weekly*, regarding the Cherry Sisters' seven years of touring.

Courtesy of Wikimedia Commons

Olympia Music Hall, was in tremendous debt. He needed something to save his theater, and thought, "I've been putting on the best talent, and it hasn't gone over. Now I'm going to try the worst!"

The Cherry Sisters were booked for eight weeks at a generous salary, and New York audiences loved every minute of the sisters' performance. Again, it was so horrible, so awful that people couldn't believe what they were seeing, and the Cherry Sisters played for over two solid months to standing-room-only crowds, saving Hammerstein's theater and making good money themselves.

For the next seven years they toured the US and Canada, and the vegetable-throwing tradition followed them. When one of the sisters died, their act did, too. They returned home and opened a bakery, making cherry pie their specialty. The Cherry Sisters never married and reportedly were never kissed. One thing is for sure: they made having no talent their talent, and it was indeed unforgettable.

Hard-Working Actor from the Heartland

Who doesn't remember goofy, loveable Michael Kelso in the retro sitcom *That 70s Show*? Or uber-rich but down-to-earth Walden Schmidt in *Two and a Half Men*? Actor Ashton Kutcher was fun to watch and always made his viewers laugh. A TV and movie star, Christopher Ashton Kutcher was born in Cedar Rapids and still comes home to visit from time to time.

He is proud of his home state, which is evidenced by how much he raves about growing up here. In 2017, he shared his feelings about the Hawkeye state with the *Des Moines Register*: "The more places I go, the more I realize how great it is here, and the more I realize that I almost owe everything of who I am to where I come from."

Kutcher was born in 1978, just minutes ahead of his fraternal twin brother, and along with their parents and sister, had a good life growing up in Cedar Rapids. In a radio interview with Kerry Washington, Kutcher said although he was "always broke," he learned about hard work in the country. He also said, "You learn how to entertain yourself when you're by yourself," sharing how he would take the initiative of learning what he was curious about or what he needed to know.

One thing he knew was that he loved acting. He loved the attention he received when he was on stage and knew he wanted to do that for a living. Acting was put aside while he was in college, though, as he majored in biochemical engineering at the University of Iowa.

While at college he was approached by a woman on campus who asked him if he had ever done any modeling. He laughed, but she persuaded him to enter a contest—which he won—and he found himself in

New York City with an agent. Although his dad urged him to come home, Kutcher stayed to pursue his dream.

Fast forward through his life when he starred in *That 70s Show*, with so many other roles afterward. He was married to Demi Moore for six years, divorced, and then married his longtime friend (and co-star of *That 70s Show*), Mila Kunis. The couple now has two children.

Kutcher's can-do attitude and hard work combined with some good luck landed him where he is today. An actor, an investor, and a philanthropist—that's Ashton Kutcher. And an Iowa boy . . . always an Iowa boy.

Ashton Kutcher always remembers his Iowa upbringing. Courtesy of JenniferJacquemart, Wikimedia Commons

What a Voice!

When Simon Estes was growing up, his family didn't have an abundance of material wealth, but he certainly received an overflowing of love and attention from them, which made him wealthier by far.

Growing up in Centerville, Estes and his siblings lived with their parents in a tiny home with no running water or electricity. His father never learned to read or write, but both of his parents instilled in their children the importance of study and a good education. Estes thought he might be a doctor someday, as he looked up to the doctors, ministers, and teachers in the community. However, being deeply religious and finding his voice in church, he sang his first solo at Centerville's Second Baptist Church as a boy soprano, which unleashed his love of singing.

He continued to sing throughout his school years, that angelic soprano voice soon turning into a powerful bass-baritone. Although he found singing very natural and easy, he still planned to study medicine and perhaps just sing on the side.

Estes attended the University of Iowa and didn't make it into the school's 300-voice choir. Instead, he joined the Old Gold Singers, a campus pop singing group. A voice teacher in the music department, Charles Kellis, heard this exceptionally talented bass-baritone and asked if he was interested in opera. "What's opera?" Estes asked. Kellis played some examples of opera singers; Estes became hooked, and Kellis became his first and only voice teacher.

Next up: studying at the famed Juilliard School of Music in New York City and making a career move to Germany, winning roles in opera and vocal competitions. Estes won the silver medal in the first international Tchaikovsky music competition in Moscow and has performed with virtually all of the major opera companies of the world. In 1982 he made his debut at the Metropolitan Opera.

Over his 50-plus-year singing career, Estes has sung for presidents, popes, and internationally renowned figures, and yet he once remarked he has felt even more honor when singing for elderly residents in nursing homes across the state of Iowa. A humble man from humble beginnings, his favorite quotation is "Let's love each other as neighbors." It's only fitting that Simon Estes's thoughts about singing can be summed up in one sentence: "In music, the only color should be the voice."

For a man who once questioned what opera was, Simon Estes later sang in many of them around the world. Courtesy of Wikimedia Commons

Big Band Man

Born in Clarinda, Iowa, Glenn Miller milked cows to earn his first musical instrument, a trombone. It was that instrument that helped him become America's premier bandleader.

Miller played in his high school band in Fort Collins, Colorado, and after graduating he played professionally, becoming a member of an orchestra. After a stint in college he went back to the music business, working with different bands, and he finally landed a spot as the musical director in Tommy Dorsey's band. Throughout his life, he moved around a lot, from Iowa to Nebraska, Missouri, Colorado, the West Coast, and finally New York City, where he arranged music for a number of orchestras.

Miller organized a band that became the most popular one in America, having the tonal balance that he sought for an ensemble effect, a blend that had a distinctive sound and a different style. This was the band that

Glenn Miller and the instrument that helped him find fame and fortune. Courtesy of Wikimedia Commons

finally put him on the map. Glenn Miller and his orchestra became well known for songs such as "Moonlight Serenade," "Tuxedo Junction," "Pennsylvania 6-5000," and of course, "In the Mood."

In 1942, at the height of the band's popularity, Miller put his successful music career aside and accepted a position in the Army Air Force in World War II. He formed a 50-piece US Army Air Force Band and gave hundreds of performances to entertain the troops. The band was a sensation, playing in packed airplane hangars, hospitals, and airstrips. It duplicated the sound he was known for, and while stationed in England, he shared that sound with GIs lonely for home. It was said that other than a letter from home, Miller's band was the greatest morale builder for the troops.

On December 15, 1944, Miller took off in a small plane headed for Paris to make arrangements for his band to present a new series of concerts. The plane was never heard from again, and America's premier bandleader disappeared without a trace. After a search for several days, the announcement was made on Dec. 24 and made newspaper headlines on Christmas Day that year.

Glenn Miller, musical giant of his day, was gone, and his loss was akin to the more recent sudden deaths of John Lennon, Michael Jackson, or Prince. What happened to his plane remains a mystery to this day.

Glenn Miller and His Top 10 Hits

Glenn Miller had 69 Top 10 Hits, which was only five less than Elvis Presley (40) and the Beatles (34) combined. What were some favorites? Odds are good you've heard a few.

Moonlight Serenade
Rhapsody in Blue
Over the Rainbow
Blueberry Hill
When You Wish Upon a Star

Tuxedo Junction
String of Pearls
At Last
In The Mood
Pennsylvania 6-5000

Courtesy of Wikimedia Commons

Snap, Crackle, Pop Treats

If you're a fan of Kellogg's Rice Krispies Treats, you have Mildred Day to thank for inventing them! Day was born Harriet Mildred Ghrist and preferred to be called Millie. She lived with her family on a farm in Durham (near Knoxville) and later relocated to Quebec, Iowa.

Great at spelling, Millie was asked to put her writing skills to use at a newspaper when her family moved to Ames when she was in high school. She continued to write in college at Iowa State University, where she majored in home economics and met her future husband, James Meredith Day.

Before she received her diploma, Millie had secured a job with Kellogg's Cereal Company in Battle Creek, Michigan. James Day proposed, and she had to ask permission from Kellogg's to work there as a future married woman. Kellogg's agreed, and the couple was married. Living very frugally as newlyweds, they ate at home for most of their meals. James told people, "Why should we eat out when Millie can cook better than anyone at a restaurant?"

Being a good cook came in handy with Millie's job. At Kellogg's, she tested recipes and was in charge of cooking schools in 38 states. After the popularity of the company's new cereal, Rice Krispies, she and a coworker, Malitta Jensen, created the Rice Krispies Treat. Earlier recipes for the treat square used puffed rice or puffed wheat and molasses. It was Millie who thought that marshmallows would be less messy than molasses, and tastier, too!

Six months later, the Camp Fire girls association called Kellogg's asking for fundraising ideas. Kellogg's decided to test-run their "marshmallow squares," and Millie was put on a train to Kansas City. Armed with her

Mildred Day not only invented Rice Krispie Treats but also made them for most everyone . . . except her daughter! Courtesy of Wikimedia Commons

huge baking trays and giant mixer, she worked very long days making batch after batch of the treats for the fundraiser.

Kellogg's put the recipe for Rice Krispies Treats on their cereal boxes for the first time in 1941, and the beauty of the treat was that people could make them at home. When Millie's daughter, Sandra, found out later in life that her own mother had invented these treats, she asked her mother why she had never made them for her as a child. Millie's answer? "If you'd made them for two weeks from 6:30 in the morning until 10:30 at night, you wouldn't want to make them again, either."

Keokuk's Writing Son

Keokuk can claim Samuel Clemens (aka Mark Twain) as its son, if only for a couple of short years.

Before Clemens acquired his pen name and became a legendary author, he followed his older brother, Orion, to Muscatine in the summer of 1853. He had been writing for his brother's newspaper, the Muscatine *Journal*, as a correspondent. He wrote about his experiences in Muscatine later in *Life on the Mississippi* and was especially impressed by the sunsets, saying, "I have never seen any, on either side of the ocean, that equaled them."

He moved away for more training in journalism, but returned to Iowa in 1854, this time to Keokuk. Once again he worked for his brother, who had just bought a new printing business. Clemens made a whole $5 a week at this job. He and his brothers, Orion and Henry, put together the first City Directory, made available to Keokuk residents for $1 each. Most of the type for the directory was set by Clemens, who listed himself in its pages as an "antiquarian." When asked the reason for this, he replied that he always thought every town should have at least one antiquarian, and since no one had appeared for the post, he decided to volunteer!

It was in Keokuk that Clemens achieved two firsts: (1) he received his first earnings for his writing, and (2) he started his speaking career. He gave his first after-dinner speech at a printers' banquet, and the local newspaper raved over his wit and humor, which caused the audience to interrupt him with long bursts of applause.

He left the area in 1857 to become a steamboat pilot on the Mississippi, and he didn't return until 1869, when he came back as Mark Twain to lecture in Keokuk, Davenport, and Iowa City.

Mark Twain's writing was homespun and stemmed from his early days in Iowa.
Courtesy of Wikimedia Commons

Iowa's weather seems to have made a big impact on Clemens. First, the sunsets in Muscatine, and then the heat and the cold of Iowa found their way into his writing, including a letter that he wrote to his mother in 1886. "The heat was so extreme it could make a person cry," he wrote. And in his autobiography, he recalled the "bitter winter" of 1856 in Keokuk.

He also wrote about people he met while in Iowa, including a gentleman by the name of Thomas Sawyer. Sound familiar?

Just Like Nancy Drew

The first person ever to receive a master's degree from the University of Iowa in the School of Journalism in 1927 also happens to be the author of 23 of the first 30 Nancy Drew books! Mildred Wirt Benson, born in Ladora in 1905, wrote as "Carolyn Keene," and by many other pen names for different series over the years.

Translated into 26 languages, Nancy Drew books are about a teenage sleuth who has a spunky personality and courage galore. A treasured literary heroine, Nancy Drew offered many their first foray into mysteries. The books were written for a reading level of ages eight to 12; however, the stories appeal to young and old alike.

Just two years after graduate school, Mildred received a slim outline from New York's Stratemeyer Syndicate with a request to ghost-write a mystery novel (for $125 and no royalties) about a girl named Nancy Drew. She wrote the very first book in the series, *The Secret of the Old Clock*, as well as books 2–7, 11–25 and 30 . . . out of a total of 56 titles, which were all written by ghostwriters such as Mildred over the years. Currently, over 80 million Nancy Drew books have been sold since the first one in 1930, and many other titles have also been added beyond the original classic series.

Mildred also wrote other series and children's books—135 in all, delighting millions with her prolific writing through the years. In fact she published her first story, "The Courtesy," in *St. Nicholas* when she was only 13.

Jennifer Fisher, an author and consultant and the president of Nancy Drew Sleuths, has spent over a decade researching the impact that Mildred (and Nancy Drew) had on readers over the years. She was fortunate to have met Mildred and shared: "Mildred Wirt Benson was a real-life Nancy Drew—or Nancy Drew was Mildred Wirt Benson!

Mildred Wirt Benson surrounded by some of her books, including many of the Nancy Drew mystery series, which she wrote as a ghostwriter, Carolyn Keene. Courtesy of the *Toledo Blade* via the *Toledo Times*, published August 10, 1949

She had a zest for adventure and loved to write. She took up flying and archaeology years after writing Nancy Drew and many other series and books. She once thought, 'What would Nancy Drew Do (or WWNDD)?' when she was kidnapped in Guatemala on an archaeology trip and got herself out of the situation . . . much like Nancy Drew might have. [Mildred] was inquisitive, bold, tenacious, and very intelligent . . . just like Nancy Drew!"

The Lawnmower Man

Driving 240 miles to see a brother doesn't usually make the news, but when the vehicle of choice is a lawnmower, it's pretty newsworthy. Alvin Straight of Laurens was 73 when he heard his 80-year-old brother, Henry, had suffered a stroke in Mount Zion, Wisconsin. The two brothers hadn't spoken in years, and Alvin wasn't sure how much time was left.

Alvin wasn't in the best of health himself. He suffered from diabetes, emphysema, and poor eyesight. His vision was so poor that he couldn't hold a driver's license. Since he didn't trust anyone else to drive him to Wisconsin, he decided to drive himself . . . on his riding lawn mower.

He didn't just jump on his lawn mower and start his journey; he prepared for it by giving it a tune-up and loading supplies and camping gear on a small trailer attached behind it. He set out on July 5, 1994—and only 30 miles down the road, his lawn mower gave out on him.

After he was towed home, he bought an old John Deere riding mower and set out again. This time, he made it almost 35 miles before breaking down. He had the mower fixed while he camped out on someone's lawn, and soon he was back in business, driving for hours a day on the

No car? No money? No problem. Alvin Straight drove a John Deere riding lawn mower (such as this) across Iowa to visit his brother. Courtesy of Wikimedia Commons

shoulder of the Iowa highway. This was where he set up camp nightly as well, cooking, eating, and sleeping in his little trailer on the side of the road.

By the time he got to Charles City, about 133 miles from Laurens, he had run out of money and had to stay in town until his next Social Security check reached his account. Now more than halfway to Henry's house, he took off once more, heading on Iowa's Highway 18 and crossing over the Mississippi River by Marquette. Smooth sailing (or riding) until the next breakdown, which happened only two miles away from his brother. It was only then that he accepted help from a farmer who volunteered to push his mower the rest of the way.

The 240-mile trip took Alvin six weeks, and he stayed with Henry and his wife for a few weeks while Henry recovered from his stroke. The brothers reconciled and later even frequented local bars together . . . on a riding lawn mower.

Give It to Me Straight

News of Alvin's unique journey traveled around the world, even in the days before social media. Talk shows like *The Tonight Show with Jay Leno* and *The Late Show with David Letterman* asked Alvin to be a guest on their shows. He turned them down.

And then Hollywood came calling. Filmmaker David Lynch re-created the journey in *The Straight Story*, starring Richard Farnsworth, Sissy Spacek, and Harry Dean Stanton. The movie was uncharacteristic for Lynch, and yet it was well received for being pure and simple . . . just like Alvin Straight.

Buffalo Bill's Wild West

The Wild West. Cowboys. Roping cattle. Hunting buffalo. These images can conjure up only one famous Iowan: William F. Cody, more commonly known as "Buffalo Bill." Born in LeClaire in 1846, Bill began his schooling there but found he was more attracted to swimming in the Mississippi and riding horses. Before he was 10 he found that his talents lay in outdoor adventures. He was equally at home on a horse, shooting at anything, roping a calf, or driving a team of horses.

The Cody family moved to Kansas in 1853, which was a turning point in Bill's life. When his father was killed for speaking out against slavery, Bill was left as the man of the house, so he joined the Pony Express to support his family.

"Buffalo Bill" put on a circus Wild-West style. Courtesy of Wikimedia Commons

He served as a scout for the Union Army in the Civil War and killed buffalo for the railroad laborers, once even entering a buffalo-killing contest. With his one-day total of 69 buffalo killed, he earned the prize money of $500 and the name, "Buffalo Bill."

Several more adventurous jobs such as cattle herder, justice of the peace, cattle baron, and Nebraska legislator made him the ultimate plainsman, and he became quite famous locally. After a dime novelist named Ned Buntline wrote a series of "larger than life" stories about him, Buffalo Bill became a national celebrity.

He had the idea to exhibit the fading way of life in the "Wild West" in a show he presented to people in the Eastern US and Europe. Full of excitement comparable to a circus, but "Western style" with horse-riding, cattle-roping, and mock battles, this Wild West Show was wildly successful, and Buffalo Bill made a fortune from it. He performed in his last Wild West Show in Davenport in 1913, and four years later, he died while visiting his sister in Denver, Colorado. His gravesite is on Lookout Mountain near Golden, Colorado, a site with spectacular views of both mountains and plains. The Buffalo Bill Museum near his gravesite is dedicated to Buffalo Bill's life . . . which began in Iowa.

Annie Oakley was a sharpshooter featured in *Buffalo Bill's Wild West Show*. The musical *Annie Get Your Gun* is based on her time in his show. Courtesy of Buffalo Bill Museum

He's a Music Man

Meredith Willson can be summed up in 10 words: "He's a music man. He's a what? He's a what?" If you've either seen or acted in a production of *The Music Man,* you'll recognize this from the infamous "Rock Island" train scene of the musical that Meredith Willson wrote as "an Iowan's attempt to pay tribute to his home state."

Meredith Willson was a musician famous for his musicals, school songs, and Christmas tunes. Courtesy of Wikimedia Commons

Born in 1902, Meredith weighed over 14 pounds, which made him the largest baby born in Iowa at the time. He was setting records from the time he was born. Meredith was the baby of the family, with an older sister, Dixie, and older brother, Cedric, both of whom also ended up being high achievers in life.

All three Willson kids played the piano because their mother, Rosalie, taught it in their home.

Rosalie was a stickler for practice, making sure that her kids spent time perfecting their piano exercises. She told Meredith, "If you're going to play an instrument, you need to be good at it so as to stand out from the other boys."

Willson played the flute and piccolo at Mason City High School, then took off for New York City after graduating and attended the prestigious Damrosch Institute of Musical Art (which would later become the Julliard School). After graduation, he played with the concert bandmaster John Philip Sousa and later the New York Philharmonic. He began conducting and composing until World War II broke out and he enlisted. When the war ended in 1945, Willson entertained once again on network radio.

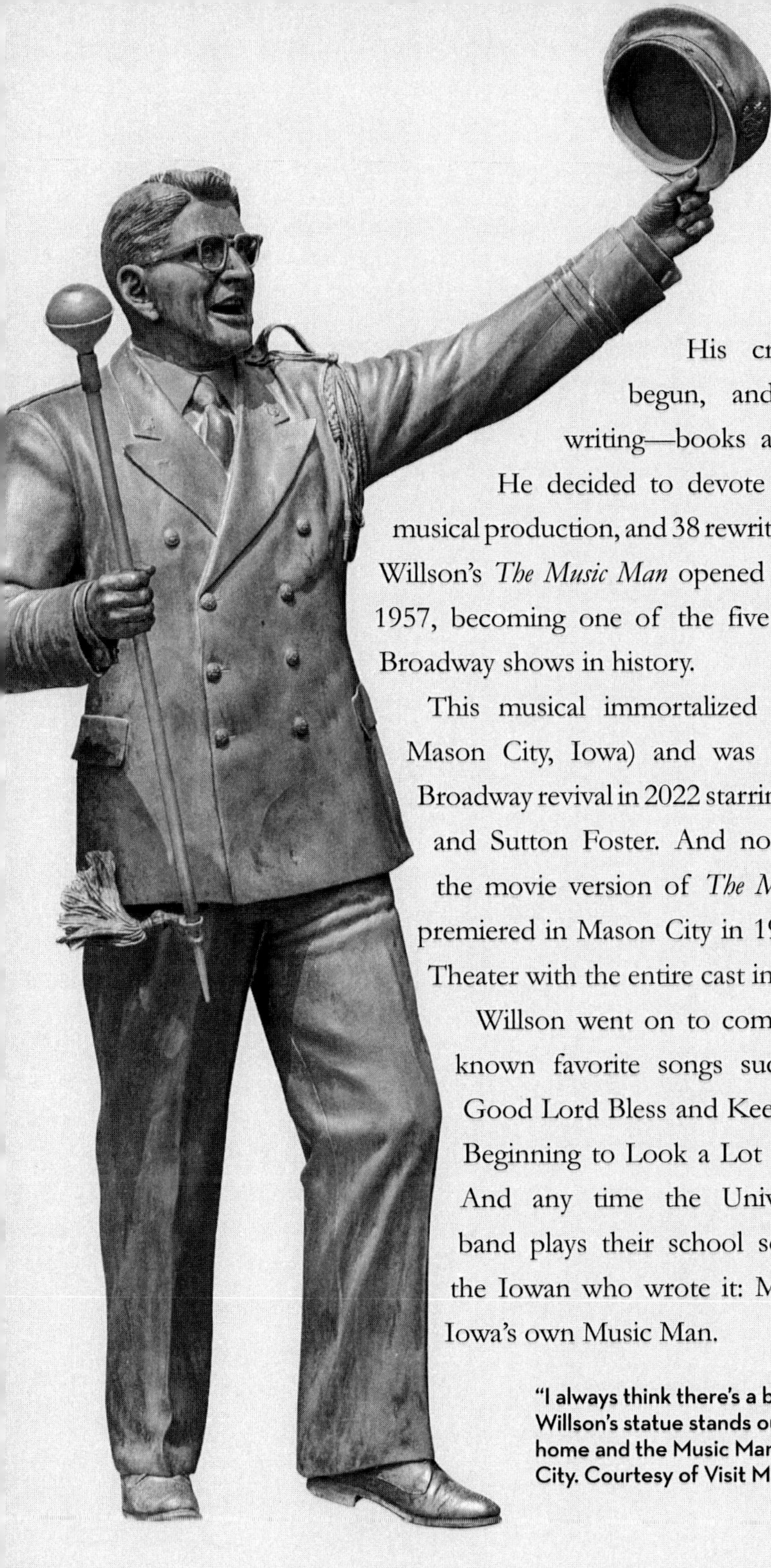

His creative era had begun, and Willson kept writing—books as well as songs. He decided to devote his efforts to a musical production, and 38 rewrites later, Meredith Willson's *The Music Man* opened on Broadway in 1957, becoming one of the five longest-running Broadway shows in history.

This musical immortalized River City (aka Mason City, Iowa) and was most recently a Broadway revival in 2022 starring Hugh Jackman and Sutton Foster. And no one can forget the movie version of *The Music Man,* which premiered in Mason City in 1962 at the Palace Theater with the entire cast in attendance.

Willson went on to compose other well-known favorite songs such as "May the Good Lord Bless and Keep You" and "It's Beginning to Look a Lot Like Christmas." And any time the University of Iowa band plays their school song, they honor the Iowan who wrote it: Meredith Willson, Iowa's own Music Man.

"I always think there's a band, kid!" Meredith Willson's statue stands outside his boyhood home and the Music Man Square in Mason City. Courtesy of Visit Mason City

More than OK

Wyatt Earp was rambunctious when he was young. As an adult, he used that experience to control others just like him. Courtesy of Wikimedia Commons

Wyatt Earp, the last surviving participant of the OK Corral shootout, spent around 14 years in Pella. He came to town with his family in 1850 when he was two, lived there until he was around 15, and ran away to join the Army. Ironically, he was sent back home to Pella by his father, an Army officer.

Growing up in Pella with plenty of siblings, younger and older, Wyatt was never at a loss for someone to "raise a ruckus" with him. Historical accounts tell stories about how the Earp boys liked to fight, with each other and also with the local Dutch. One story tells about how Wyatt was "clobbered" with another boy's wooden shoe in one such fight. (It turns out wooden shoes weren't only worn for looks back in the day.)

Wyatt did in his mid-teens what most wouldn't have dreamed of even as adults. He drove a team of horses to California for his father to prospect for gold. He drove a stagecoach over a route repeatedly robbed by thieves. He provided meat for railroad gangs. Soon he was a wealthy man.

He moved west and became a frontier marshal in Wichita, Kansas, as he was known as a sober and honest man, and the townspeople begged him to control the outlaws who tried to take over their town. Wyatt went on to be marshal in Dodge City, Kansas, and Tombstone, Arizona, and never once did he lose a fight. During his time in Tombstone, the Earps and Wyatt's friend "Doc" Holliday had run-ins with some area outlaws, culminating in a big confrontation at the OK Corral in October 1881. Some were killed; some were injured; Wyatt was untouched.

From that time on, Wyatt wandered around the western states and dabbled at different jobs for the rest of his life. Besides buying and selling horses, refereeing boxing matches, and getting into mining, Wyatt went to Los Angeles and acted as a consultant on western silent movies, meeting many people, including another Iowan, a young prop boy by the name of Marion Morrison, who later became known as John Wayne. It's a small world indeed.

Home Sweet Row House

For three of their years in Pella, the Earp family lived in the Van Spancheren Row Houses, which were built in 1850 and housed several apartments and businesses. Their apartment was on the east side of the house. Today, this building is on the National Register of Historic Places and has been restored to what it looked like in that earlier era. The Pella Historical Society bought the building, and it became the first in their now 20-building Historical Village.

The Earp family's apartment can be toured in Pella's Historical Village.

Advice Queens

Pauline Phillips, also known as "Dear Abby." Courtesy of Wikimedia Commons

Before the days of reality TV and social media, and during a time when physical copies of newspapers and magazines were read cover to cover, people couldn't get enough of advice columns. They wrote to advice columnists for help with their own problems, and for entertainment they'd read about the problems of others. Advice columns provided answers to all sorts of questions, and they sparked great conversations on sometimes controversial topics.

Eppie Lederer, also known as "Ann Landers." Courtesy of Wikimedia Commons

Twin sisters from Sioux City became the most-read women in world history because of their advice columns. These sisters were Esther P. and Pauline E. Friedman, born on the Fourth of July in 1918. Esther P. became known as advice columnist Ann Landers of "Ask Ann" fame, while twin Pauline E. became Abigail Van Buren, aka "Dear Abby." Friends and family just nicknamed them Eppie and Popo.

The twins were inseparable while they were growing up in Sioux City. Their parents had emigrated from Russia 10 years before they were born, and by the time the twins were in school their father owned three theaters downtown. Their house was the place to be for vaudeville performers, and the girls loved to ask them for advice and hear their "juicy stories" of the world outside of Iowa.

Of course, Eppie and Popo took what they learned from the performers and regaled their junior high classmates with the sometimes-steamy info they had learned from the chorus girls at their house.

The twin bond they had growing up didn't end after high school, as both attended Morningside College and were even married in a dual wedding ceremony. Eppie moved to Chicago and won a contest at the *Sun-Times* to be the replacement advice columnist for "Ann Landers." Popo moved to San Francisco and talked the editor of the *San Francisco Chronicle* into trying a sample advice column, which of course became a full-blown one after "Dear Abby's" success. Both "Ann" and "Abigail" received accolades galore, and even more than that, the love of a nation for their homespun Iowa advice.

Abby's Words of Wisdom

Twin sisters, but very different advice styles. Ann Landers was "homey" while Abby was "flippant."

Dear Abby: My boyfriend is going to be 20 next month. I'd like to give him something nice for his birthday. What do you think he'd like?—Carol

Dear Carol: Never mind what he'd like; give him a tie.

Dear Abby: I've been going with this girl for a year. How can I get her to say yes?—Don

Dear Don: What's the question?

Dear Abby star on the Hollywood Walk of Fame. Courtesy of Wikimedia Commons

We Stick Together

A parent of a child in the service is never ready for a visit from an official with the worst possible news. Imagine the heartbreak that Thomas and Alleta Sullivan of Waterloo went through when they found out all five of their sons were tragically killed while serving on their ship, the USS *Juneau*, on November 13, 1942. The death of the brothers was the biggest blow to any one family in US wartime history.

The five Sullivan brothers, George, Francis, Joseph, Madison, and Albert, all joined the Navy in World War II after their friend from Fredericksburg died on the USS *Arizona* at Pearl Harbor. They joined with the stipulation that all five of them would be able to serve together, which was a departure from Navy policy.

The Sullivan brothers on board the USS *Juneau* on February 14, 1942: Joe, Frank, Al, Matt, and George. Courtesy of groutmuseumdistrict.org

The USS *Juneau*, along with other US warships, was hit by a torpedo in the Battle for Guadalcanal, which caused the ship to sink in just 42 seconds. Four of the Sullivan brothers couldn't make it topside in time to abandon the ship. Already wounded, George managed to pull himself onto a raft but died hours later due to his wounds. Surviving family members included their parents; their sister, Genevieve; and the youngest brother's wife and son, Katherine and Jimmy Sullivan.

News of the tragedy traveled around the world. The fallen brothers were honored with two ships named after them, the USS *The Sullivans* (DD-537) and USS *The Sullivans* (DDG-68). Their motto is "We Stick Together," just as the Sullivan brothers were famous for saying.

In 1944, the movie *The Sullivans* was released, based on the true story of the five brothers. Many years later, in 1998, the movie *Saving Private Ryan* was released, also inspired by the real-life story of the Sullivans. Directed by Steven Spielberg, *Saving Private Ryan* won an Oscar, and Spielberg acknowledged their sacrifice when accepting the award.

Their hometown of Waterloo has also honored the Sullivan brothers on several occasions. In 1964 Sullivan Park was dedicated on the site of the family home, and in 1988 a convention center was named after them. In 2008, the Grout Museum District opened the Sullivan Brothers Iowa Veterans Museum, dedicated to all Iowans who served our nation.

The Great Humanitarian

President Herbert Hoover had a great quote that still rings true to any parent of boys. "Boys are very durable. A boy, if not washed too often and if kept in a cool dry place after each accident, will survive broken bones, hornets' nests, swimming holes and five helpings of pie." And likewise for parents of girls: "But sooner or later she is sure to meet a spirit equally as independent as her own, and then—there is a clash of arms ending in mortal combat, or they unite their forces and with combined strength go forth to meet the world."

Hoover's pride in his home state is evident in this memorable passage from the end of an informal address he gave as president before the Iowa Society of Washington, DC, in 1927: "There are few scars that people carry from the State of Iowa. The good Lord originally made it the richest stretch of agricultural land that ever blessed any one sovereign government. It was populated by the more adventurous and the more courageous, who fought their way along the ever-extending frontier. They builded here in so short a period as 75 years a people who today enjoy the highest standard of living, the highest average intelligence, the highest average degree of education that has ever blessed a single commonwealth. There is no man or woman born of Iowa who is not proud of his native state."

Hoover was born in 1874 in West Branch, Iowa, and was sent to live with an uncle in Oregon after his parents' death when he was 10 years old. He went to Stanford University at 17 years old and met fellow Iowan Lou Henry, whom he later married. Hoover was appointed chief mining engineer for the Chinese government in 1899. Fifteen years later, when 10 million Belgians were starving during World War I, Hoover helped to deliver $1 billion worth of food for them. A bowl of soup and a piece of bread came to be called a "Hoover lunch" by grateful Belgian children.

When the US entered World War I, President Woodrow Wilson asked Hoover to head the US Food Administration. Hoover accepted, asking for total control and no pay. Monikers such as "The Great Humanitarian" were bestowed upon Hoover, and after being secretary of commerce under president Warren G. Harding, Hoover became 31st president of the United States in 1929.

There are 15 presidential libraries in the United States, and the one in West Branch is dedicated to Iowa-born Herbert Hoover, the last great humanitarian.

President Herbert Hoover was born in West Branch and was always proud of his state. Courtesy of the Library of Congress

The American Duke

Think of John Wayne and picture the ultimate cowboy . . . or at least one who appeared in Western movies for a career spanning around 40 years. Born in Winterset in 1907, "John's" real name was Marion Morrison, and he had Midwestern roots from the start. He was the son of a pharmacist who worked in a local drugstore. Because his dad developed some heart issues, a physician recommended that the family move to a drier climate, so they headed out west to California. It was in California where his well-known nickname "Duke" originated.

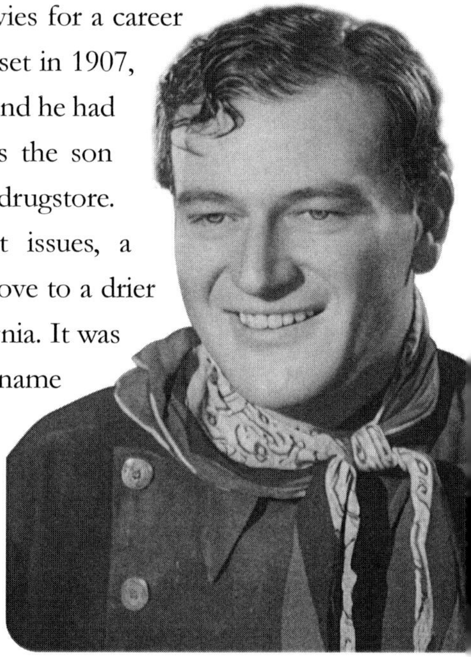

Young John Wayne in the 1930s. Courtesy of John Wayne Birthplace & Museum

Marion was often seen walking Duke, his Airedale Terrier, past the fire station, and a local fireman began calling Marion "Little Duke." The name stuck and evolved into just "Duke." The Duke's neighbors were in the movie business, so he and some football teammates decided to try it out. He started working in film studios as a prop boy (and met Wyatt Earp, also from Iowa) and appeared in at least 20 movies without credit (or as Marion Morrison).

One day, the Duke was spotted and awarded the starring role in the 1930 movie *The Big Trail.* The film director suggested a name change, and Marion became known as John Wayne. In 1939 he became the leading man in the hit movie *Stagecoach.* He had swagger, steady work, and screen exposure. The Duke worked on his demeanor and speech mannerisms on and off screen, and this (along with a great script) helped him win an Academy Award for his role in *True Grit.* Who would've thought of all of his roles that this one—as the drunken, overweight, one-eyed sheriff—would be the one that would win him the most acclaim?

The eyepatch that the Duke wore in *True Grit* now sits in the John Wayne Birthplace Museum, a 6,100-square-foot building in Winterset that houses a huge collection of memorabilia from his life, personal and professional. (Interestingly, the eyepatch he wore in the movie was see-through so he could watch what others were doing on set.)

The ultimate cowboy, John Wayne, rose to fame from a humble beginning in Iowa. Courtesy of John Wayne Birthplace & Museum

After a bout with cancer and heart disease, even the Duke wasn't strong enough to fight. He died at age 72. The day after he died, the US Congress voted to award him its highest honor, even though he had never served in the armed forces. This honor, the Congressional Gold Medal, was inscribed simply and suitably, with this: John Wayne—American.

Mr. State Fair

Perhaps no other father and son in Iowa are as revered as the "original" Mr. State Fair, Bill Riley Sr. who started the Bill Riley Talent Show at the Iowa State Fair, and his son, Bill Riley Jr., who carries on his father's legacy with the same enthusiasm as his dad.

Bill Riley Sr., used to emcee variety shows held at the Iowa State Fair by KRNT radio starting in 1946. A little over a decade later, Bill asked the fair secretary if he could showcase talented kids during the fair. A couple of years later he held his first talent search, and beginning in 1959, he was traveling across the state holding talent shows. The best of the best would later compete at the Iowa State Fair, just as they do now.

His love of finding talent in kids ages 2 to 21 and promoting it at the fair got him his nickname, "Mr. State Fair." He retired in 1996, and the stage at the fairgrounds was renamed the Bill Riley Stage. Bill celebrated his 60th fair in 2006 and passed away later that year.

It was a good thing his son, Bill Riley Jr., had been helping his dad since 1996 and was ready to go from being the understudy to the leading man. Bill Jr. didn't plan to follow in his father's footsteps; instead, he "tried to be cool." He had no radio, TV, or public-speaking experience, but he learned.

While his father was still alive, he shared nuggets of wisdom with his son. Bill Jr. said, "Dad was a great cheerleader. If you messed up, he was one of those parents that picked you up, kicked you in the rear, and said, 'Get back up there and keep going!'"

He also learned something right before he went onstage in Iowa Falls to emcee his very first talent show. "Mr. State Fair" told his son, "Never turn your back on the act!" Bill Jr. explained that this not only shows support but also keeps the spotlight on the performers.

Bill Riley Jr. poses behind a statue of his father with two dancers, Matt Zittritch and Elyssa (Wilson) Allison, competing in the Bill Riley Talent Show in Iowa Falls. Courtesy of Barb Wilson

After all those years behind the scenes and now running the show, Bill Jr. admits he still gets butterflies before going onstage. "If you don't have butterflies, you better check something!" he stressed.

Bill Riley Jr. had big shoes to fill, but he certainly accomplished it. And Iowans couldn't be more proud of him.

Heroine on the Rails

Kate Shelley saved lives while risking her own—at the age of 15. Courtesy of Wikimedia Commons

This story has all the makings of a blockbuster movie. A teenage girl. A raging storm. A speeding train in danger of plunging off a high bridge and killing all of its passengers if not warned in time. To top things off, it was July 6, 1881, way before a quick phone call or text could have saved the day.

Kate Shelley was that real-life teenager. She was 17 at the time and used to a life of hardship. She and her family had immigrated to the United States from Ireland and settled on a homestead near Honey Creek in Boone County. Her father took a railroad job to supplement his income as a farmer, so the family soon became accustomed to the sights and sounds of trains. Tragically, her father died, leaving Kate with her mother and four younger siblings. As the oldest child, Kate took on extra responsibility . . . more than she ever thought possible.

When a violent storm hit their area that night in 1881, she and her mother heard a train crossing the Honey Creek bridge, along with its bells, the hissing of steam, and a terrible crash as the engine plunged into the

stream below. Since Kate knew that the Midnight Limited train was on its way, *on that same track*, she wanted to warn them. If she didn't, who would? And if the train wasn't warned when it stopped in Moingona, it would face that same fate.

Kate was compelled to venture out in the storm and make her way across the broken parts of the long, high Des Moines River Bridge, a daring feat even during daylight in perfect weather.

The railroad was aware of the danger of this high bridge, and to discourage trespassers, they had removed some of the bridge's flooring, leaving wide gaps between the ties.

Kate made her way on her hands and knees, the only way that she could avoid being blown off the bridge entirely. She carried her father's lantern to light her way . . . until the wind blew it out. Miraculously, she made it to the depot in Moingona, arriving in time for an agent to flag down the train and save many lives.

News of Kate's heroic actions spread quickly. In addition to national notoriety, Kate was showered with gifts and awards.

Today, a railroad bridge in the area is named in honor of Kate, who remained in Boone County working for the railroad. Never married, she died in 1912, but she remains a heroine of the high bridge.

The Kate Shelley High Bridge is one of the highest and longest double-track bridges in the US. Completed in 1901, the old bridge stands next to the new one.

The uniquely laid bricks and beautiful surroundings of Snake Alley are just as interesting as Burlington's zigzagging road.

Chapter Three

Iowa Curiosities and Oddities

There's a saying in journalism, "When a dog bites a man, that's not news, but when a man bites a dog, it *is* news!" Iowa doesn't have a lot of people going around biting dogs, but there have been many fun and unusual stories in this state's history.

One booming coal mining town in the early 1900s was a huge success in promoting diversity and inclusivity before its time, and today all that remains of it are the stories. Another town exists on an island . . . in the middle of the country. And still another town boasts the crookedest street in the world, pulling some of the thunder from San Francisco to the Midwest.

Hiccups that last for years. A huge geyser lasting longer than its surprised town was prepared for. Monks who make a living preparing for people to die. Sound strange? Oh, there's more. Prisoners of war doing something nice for their captors. A trail that glows in the dark. A church that was built almost to a songwriter's specifications, only the songwriter never shared the song.

Sometimes truth is stranger than fiction. It certainly is in Iowa.

Iowa's "Black Utopia"

Over 100 years ago, a mining town named Buxton was a thriving community in southeastern Iowa. Today, it would be difficult to find any evidence of a town ever having been there at all. Although there are many "ghost towns" in Iowa today, Buxton remains one of the most famous. It offered something unique for its time: racial integration and harmony, especially in an era when racial tolerance was the exception and not the rule.

Buxton was established by the Consolidation Coal Company (CCC) in 1900 by a man named J. E. Buxton. When the company struggled to find workers for its mines, it began to recruit Black workers from southern states. This wouldn't have been so unique in itself, but the fact that both Black and White workers received the same pay and benefits, lived and worked alongside one another, and sent their children to integrated schools—this was quite something. In fact, Buxton was considered by many to be a Black utopia.

Buxton was a booming mining town and quickly became known as one of the largest coal mining towns west of the Mississippi. By 1905, Buxton's citizens consisted of 2,700 Black residents and 1,991 White residents. The CCC built schools, parks, and other establishments, and all residents had the opportunity to open their own businesses if they

Center Street of Buxton (ca. 1908) was also called "coal chute hill" as the coal was moved from railroad cars at the bottom of the hill to the coal conveyor and chute at the top. Courtesy of State Historical Society of Iowa

so desired. Black doctors, lawyers, and other professionals prospered because of the opportunities provided here. Two notable citizens included Buxton resident E. A. Carter, who became the first Black man to get a medical degree from the University of Iowa, and George H. Woodson, who co-founded the Niagara Movement, which eventually became the NAACP.

As World War I broke out, the demand for coal was at an all-time high, and Buxton's Black residents experienced a standard of living unheard of at the time. However, mechanization and a decreased demand for coal soon followed, the population shrunk dramatically, and the town's final mine closed in 1927.

Very little remains of Buxton today, but it's an important part of Iowa history. It was an unusual place where people were color blind, and this little town thrived because of it.

The Buxton Wonders Baseball Team

Buxton was also home to the Buxton Wonders baseball team, an integrated team that played games around Iowa, Chicago, Kansas City, and Birmingham. The team was partially sponsored by the CCC, who built bleachers and paid for the team's uniforms. For an unincorporated town that had no city council, mayor, or police, Buxton offered a lesson in an incredible journey of racial equity. Although the Buxton Wonders weren't always well-received in other towns, home games were events, and the city band often held concerts afterward.

The Buxton Wonders Baseball Team played from 1900 to 1920. Courtesy of Wikimedia Commons

POWs and a Nativity

A promise made to a German POW in World War II is still kept to this day in Algona. During World War II, Algona was one of two towns in Iowa to house thousands of German POWs at Camp Algona. While the countries were at war, the POWs were put to work to relieve the manpower shortage caused by the war. Iowa had roughly 70,000 fewer people working in agriculture than before the war began, and POWs helped to ease the strain.

Eduard Kaib, a German officer captured in France and sent to Camp Algona in the fall of 1944, missed his family as the holiday season approached and created a small nativity set with figures made of soil. This scene was displayed in the camp's dining hall and caught the eye of Camp Commander Arthur Lobdell. Lobdell asked Kaib if he'd be willing to create an even larger display for the following Christmas, and Kaib agreed, even though the project would be done at his own expense.

He enlisted five other POWs to assist him, and over the course of a year, they hand-carved plaster set upon heavy concrete-covered wood and wire frames that featured 65 one-half life-sized figures, from the Baby Jesus, Mary, Joseph, and the Wise Men to sheep and camels. They finished the project in 1945, and the Germans presented their nativity to

This nativity scene was created by POWs at Camp Algona and may be viewed only during the Christmas season. Courtesy of Algona Nativity Committee

the people of Algona. When the camp disbanded in 1946, the nativity set was left behind with three requests from Kaib: (1) It needed to stay in Algona; (2) no admission could ever be charged to view it; and (3) it could be viewed only at Christmas time.

Since that time, the nativity has been housed in a climate-controlled building on the county fairgrounds. It is taken care of by the Men's Club of the Methodist Church and is available for public viewing only during the Christmas season every year. Visitors have come to see this from all 50 states and around the world.

Silent Night in Algona

The real-life story of the nativity set and the German POWs in Algona can now be seen in the movie *Silent Night in Algona*. Writer/actor D. J. Perry learned of the story at a conference and decided to bring it to life in this "solid, Midwestern feel" of a movie. Filmed in Algona and at a historical village in nearby Forest City, *Silent Night in Algona* is a heartfelt look into a time that won't ever be forgotten.

This movie (which is now available to stream) was inspired by true events related to the Algona POW camp and was filmed in the area. Courtesy of Silent Night in Algona LLC (with thanks to DJ Perry)

Hiccups That Set a World Record

Hiccups can be so annoying if they don't go away quickly. Imagine how Anthon resident Charles Osborne felt—he had them for 68 years!

Born in 1894, Charles started hiccuping in 1922 after an incident with a hog. "I was hanging a 350-pound hog for butchering. I picked it up and then I fell down. I felt nothing, but the doctor said I busted a blood vessel the size of a pin in my brain," Charles said in a 1982 *People* magazine interview. According to his doctor, the result of his fall was that "he destroyed a small area in the brain stem that inhibits the hiccup response."

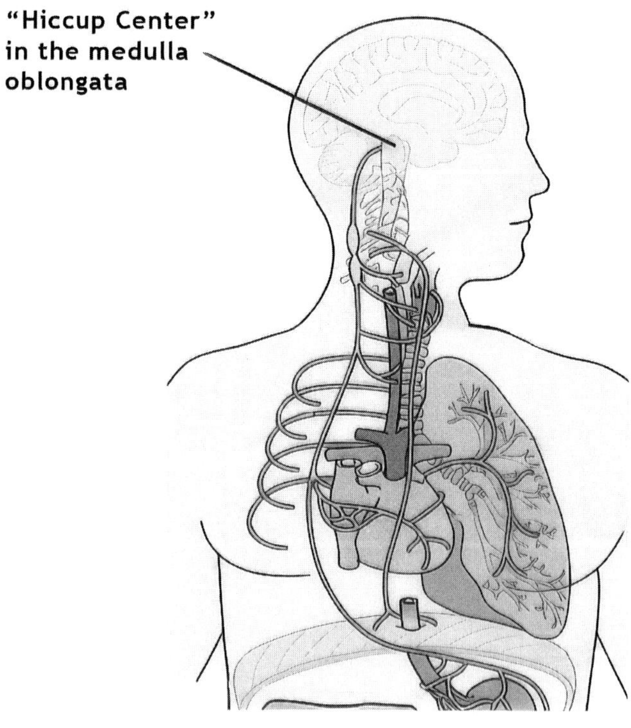

Courtesy of Wikimedia Commons

The hiccups were with him day and night at a rate of 40 times per minute. They interrupted his sleep and ruined his taste for solid food. (In later years, Charles had to grind all of his food in a blender before eating it to allow the food to "slip past the hiccups" to reach his stomach.)

He tried every remedy he could think of and sought professional treatment by several doctors, even going to the Mayo Clinic for help. Nothing worked. However, during his 21-day stay at the Mayo Clinic, the doctors there taught him a technique to suppress most of the noise by breathing between hiccups. This made the "hic" noise a little less obtrusive, but since he had to flex his chest three or four times a minute, he appeared to be "heaving," according to a friend of the family.

Charles received a lot of notoriety for his hiccups and even a bit more than "15 minutes of fame." He holds the Guinness World Record for the "longest attack of hiccups," and he appeared on such radio and TV shows as *Ripley's Believe It or Not*, *That's Incredible*! and *The Tonight Show with Johnny Carson.*

Still, he remained down to earth, according to his family and friends. Charles was married twice and had eight children. After hiccupping for 56 years, he told the Associated Press, "I'd give everything I got in the world if I could get rid of them." Then he added, "I don't know what it would be like not to have them. I get so sore jerking all the time."

Surprisingly, his hiccups suddenly stopped in 1990 . . . and he died around a year later. What an amazing hiccup-free year that must have been!

The Geyser That Wouldn't Quit

A growing town that needed more wells to provide its residents with water turned into something that no one was expecting. It was 1886, and Belle Plaine had a good problem: it was growing. More wells were being drilled all over town, until one dug by William Weir & Sons spouted water 53 feet in the air and kept on flowing for the next 14 months.

Artesian well in Belle Plaine. Courtesy of Wikimedia Commons

This was certainly the water that they were looking for, but not at all in this volume. When William Weir's company drilled on August 26, 1886, they accidentally tapped into a massive underground aquifer that created a huge geyser. It was "a whole lot of water" in Belle Plaine! In fact, it spurted and spewed more than 3,500 gallons per minute or 60 gallons per second. It was estimated that five million gallons of water flowed from the well each day.

The water just wouldn't quit. The geyser calmed down a bit and lessened its height to six to seven feet high at times, but it just kept going . . . and going . . . and going. Townspeople nicknamed it "The Old Jumbo Geyser" or "Jumbo" for short, and they also called it "The Eighth

Wonder of the World." Belle Plaine grew famous, and tourists came from around the county to see Jumbo, buying postcards and "Jumbo Well rocks."

Even with all of its newfound fame, Belle Plaine just wanted the geyser "shut off." The town hired experts from Chicago, but even they couldn't get the geyser to stop flowing. Finally, a local company, the Palmer Brothers Foundry, capped it off miraculously on October 6, 1887.

Men around the gushing well in Belle Plaine, Iowa, in the late 1890s or early 1900s. Courtesy of Calvin Photographic Collection at the University of Iowa Paleontology Repository

To put the sheer amount of water into perspective, Belle Plaine's city administrator, Stephen Beck, said in July 2024, "It was like a river flowing out of the ground." Jumbo, the geyser that took 14 months to be "tamed," is commemorated by a plaque and a huge boulder at the site where it astounded visitors galore in the late 1800s. Today it's dormant, but the giant aquifer still lies underneath the town.

The Crookedest Street in the World

Ripley's Believe It or Not calls Burlington's Snake Alley "Unbelievably Crooked," and it ranks as the #1 Odd Spot in *Ripley's Guide to the Curious Corners of America*. Some call it "the Crookedest Street in the World."

And rightly so. Snake Alley consists of five half-curves and two quarter-curves, and it drops 58 feet over a distance of 275 feet. Originally constructed in 1894 to move traffic up and down a hill too steep for a road, this "triumph of practical street engineering" also allowed for better footing for horses, as their drivers often lost control of them on steep curves. In order to accomplish this, the bricks weren't laid smoothly as on other brick roads. Instead, they were laid edge-up and beveled, requiring many more bricks.

The careful construction of this unique road connected the residential district at the top of the bluff to the commercial district at the bottom. However, horses had a difficult time climbing its curves, so the street became one-way going down, a restriction that is still in place today.

There's a legend that the Fire Department used this street as a test for horses. If a horse could take the curves at a gallup and still be breathing when it arrived at the top, it was deemed worthy and fit to haul the city's fire wagons.

This block-long zig-zagging street wasn't only functional but beautiful as well, being fashioned after vineyard paths in France and Germany. The homes surrounding the street were there before construction began and give the street an "alley-like" appearance. Located between Washington and Columbia Streets on Sixth Street in downtown Burlington, Snake Alley is on the National Register of Historic Places.

Although Snake Alley came first, San Francisco's Lombard Street, built in 1922, caused a crooked street fight. Which was more crooked?

To the naked eye, Snake Alley is slightly shorter…and there's much less traffic. Lombard Street has more turns, while Snake Alley has more extreme turns.

Snake Alley's bricks are original, and the charming street has a vintage appearance, looking almost exactly as it did in 1894. It's in a more accessible location in the heartland, and there's much less of a wait to walk or drive down. The only thing it lacks is Lombard Street's "celebrity status."

After walking (or driving) down Snake Alley, look back uphill and check out the view . . . and the *Ripley's Believe It or Not* plaque.

The oldest supper club in Iowa was loved by everyone and frequented by mobsters like Al Capone and John Dillinger. Courtesy of Google Maps

Delicious Mobster Hideout

Choose a rural location in Iowa to build a restaurant, then add some small cabins, and you have a recipe for locals to enjoy drinks and dinner and for travelers to rent a cabin without paying higher hotel tax charged within the city limits. The Lighthouse Inn Supper Club in Cedar Rapids did just that, and it also became one of the spots where you could get an illegal drink of alcohol during Prohibition.

It was also a popular stop for Chicago-area mobsters to hide out until things cooled off at home. According to the Lighthouse Inn, both Al Capone and John Dillinger dined there. At one time, a hole in the wall marked where Dillinger's gun went off. It became a part of the inn's history.

And it certainly had a long history. Established in 1912 in what was then rural Cedar Rapids, it was the oldest restaurant in that city and the second-oldest in the state. It was built on the Lincoln Highway, which opened in 1913 as the first paved highway across the United States.

Its location—"in the middle of nowhere" but still on a paved road—made it a great spot to lay low if you were someone like Al Capone.

Word has it that he was leery of driving on Iowa's gravel roads because there was a higher chance his car could get stuck in the mud. Not a good plan if a quick getaway was necessary. The Lighthouse Inn was the perfect location for him to frequent for that reason. And the food . . . you know when a mobster frequents a place, it *has* to be good!

Capone became so comfortable visiting the Lighthouse Inn that he once allegedly left a car in the parking lot. It was abandoned for so long that the restaurant's owner called the police. When they came to search the car, they found a machine gun in the trunk. It was then displayed at the police station for some time.

No mobsters visit anymore, but the stories remain.

Bittersweet End of an Era

The stories are the only things that remain at the Lighthouse Inn after August 14, 2024, when a fire broke out at the supper club. Cedar Rapids fire crews arrived at 5:20 a.m. to find the iconic restaurant fully engulfed in flames. The building is considered to be a total loss, and the cause of the fire remains under investigation. What was once a hideout for some and a second home for others is another special part of history that people will talk about for years to come.

A few weeks after the catastrophic fire at the Lighthouse Inn, considered a total loss . . .

The Day the Music Died

A ballroom that opened in 1933, burned to the ground, and relocated across the street is a story in itself. However, the Surf Ballroom in Clear Lake is most famous for an event that happened away from the property. Mention the words "the day the music died," and most people will know the reference to February 2, 1959. It was the date of the winter dance party where Buddy Holly, J. P. "The Big Bopper" Richardson, and Ritchie Valens played their last concert at the Surf before being killed in a plane crash not even five miles away.

After playing for 1,500 people at the Surf, the three performers weren't looking forward to heading to their next gig in Moorhead, Minnesota, on their freezing tour bus, so they chartered a plane. Before leaving for the Mason City airport, Holly and Valens each called home from the lobby pay phone at the Surf.

Roger Peterson, the 21-year-old pilot, had very little experience with winter flying conditions. He lost control of the small plane shortly after takeoff, and the plane crashed in a field just outside of Clear Lake, killing all four people on board.

The world of rock 'n' roll was shocked and mourned the loss of such great talent. Songwriter/performer Don McLean years later wrote a song, "American Pie," that was an homage to not only the passing of the 1950s, but also the deaths of these musicians. This is where the phrase "the day the music died" originated, and it became the song's unofficial subtitle.

In 1979, "The Mad Hatter" (aka Darryl Hensley, a Clear Lake radio personality) organized and hosted the first Buddy Holly Tribute. And every year in early February, the Surf celebrates and honors the lives of the three stars with its internationally renowned Winter Dance Party.

Step back into this timeless ballroom and experience music of the past and present. Courtesy of Surf Ballroom

The Surf Ballroom remains a very active concert venue and a museum of music greats, in particular honoring the legacy of Buddy Holly with memorabilia proudly displayed throughout the building. The Surf is listed on the National Register of Historic Places and is a National Historic Landmark.

A Place Where Music Lives On

The Surf Ballroom has made significant contributions to music history. Passionate about sharing its story and continuing its legacy, the Surf is expanding its Music Enrichment Center to provide more learning opportunities and "engage future generations in the Surf's important role in music history."

Connecting the past with the future while providing diverse learning opportunities, the Surf's $5 million expansion is underway to enhance its status as a community partner and "a place where music lives on."

Play catch or run the bases on the actual Field of Dreams in Dyersville.

Build It and They Will Come

"If you build it, he will come." This famous line from the movie *Field of Dreams* has proved true for the baseball field built in a Dyersville cornfield for the movie released in 1988 (as well as when another field was added, along with 8,000 seats for a couple of MLB games in 2021).

For anyone unfamiliar with the feel-good movie, it's about baseball and so much more. Kevin Costner starred as an Iowa farmer who has some hard luck and suddenly plows up his cornfield to build a baseball field. It's the story of fathers and sons, Midwestern values, and the joy of a good old-fashioned baseball game.

The movie is based on the book *Shoeless Joe*, by W. P. Kinsella. Filmmaker Lawrence Gordon fell in love with the story and spent years trying to get a screenplay off the ground. He finally got to move forward, and Hollywood descended on the eastern Iowa area for 68 days in the summer of 1988 to make the movie. Movie stars, professional actors, and local Iowa actors helped to make this little baseball movie magical.

After the film crew left, the now-famous field remained. The only problem was that it was built across the property line of two farmers. For two decades, they ran competing attractions only a few feet apart. Eventually one of the farmers bought out the other and the field was "united."

Visitors from all over the world came to see this movie site. Some just showed up. Others ran around the bases. Fathers and sons played catch. People sat on the bleachers where the actors did in the movie. Some treated the field as a shrine. And everyone had to run in and out of the rows of corn, just like the ghost players did in the movie.

In 2021, baseball Hall of Famer Frank Thomas and his business partners bought a controlling interest in the movie site's ownership. Their plan is to give the site an $80 million makeover, adding nine new youth ballfields. But the original field stays. You don't mess with magic.

Lights, Camera, Action!

I was one of the local Iowa actors in *Field of Dreams*, and the experience was glorious! Besides the opportunity to audition for a speaking role (and have my first screen test), I was one of the few paid extras in a "Boston" scene (actually filmed in downtown Dubuque). My younger sister reported in with me for the day and suddenly found herself whisked off into the wardrobe department. We learned firsthand what acting in a movie involved. And getting to meet Kevin Costner wasn't all bad, either.

My sister, Jennifer (Sprout) Cassutt, and I posing with "our co-star" Kevin Costner during the filming of *Field of Dreams*.

Monet's painting that was stolen, *The Fishing Boats in Front of the Cliffs at Etretat.* Courtesy of Wikimedia Commons

Missing Monet in a Mailbox

A theater group was rehearsing in Marshalltown's Fisher Community Center on an ordinary Thursday night on March 19, 1987, when a thief entered the building, cut a painting by famed French impressionist Claude Monet out of its frame, and disappeared with it. The painting was valued at $175,000 and was on loan to the Chamber of Commerce.

The painting, *Les Barques de Pêche d evant les Falaises D'Étretat* (*The Fishing Boats in Front of the Cliffs at Étretat*) was painted by Monet around 1891 and was connected to an alarm at the police station. The police arrived at the scene within minutes of the theft, but the suspect was gone. Up to that point, the painting had hung in the community center for 29 years and was part of a collection owned by the Fisher Foundation, whose chairman, J. W. "Bill" Fisher, was a patron of the arts.

Local police, the FBI, and Interpol searched for the oil painting but never had any luck until almost a year later, when the missing Monet made national headlines once again. Local postmaster in Le Grand at the time, Charles Polley, found the painting on Tuesday morning, March 8, 1988, in a drop-off mailbox. Rolled up and bound with two rubber bands, the painting was mixed in with other pieces of mail. Polley's thoughts? "I thought it was trash at first—but it sure wasn't trash," he said. "It had the look of canvas, and I looked at the edges and knew exactly what it was. You never know what a day will bring."

Postal officials and the police were called, and Lt. Darrell Templeton was in disbelief. An art expert came to town to certify the painting's authenticity, and although there was some minor damage, it was indeed the real painting.

It certainly helped that the authorities did everything they could to ensure the painting couldn't be sold anywhere. They alerted museums, art galleries, and foundations that search for stolen paintings, and Templeton thought the painting was placed into the mailbox by "a remorseful thief who found it impossible to sell the stolen masterpiece."

The Monet never went back into the collection. Instead, the insurance company sold it to a private collector, and Marshalltown's community center used the money to install a tighter security system to protect the other art housed in the Fisher Center.

Which Came First–the Song or the Church?

The song "The Church in the Wildwood," or as some call it, "The Little Brown Church in the Vale," is synonymous with this place in Nashua, the Little Brown Church. But was the song written before or after the church was built?

A young teacher, William Pitts, was traveling from his home in Wisconsin to visit his fiancée in Fredericksburg in 1857. While taking a break around Bradford, he took a little walk and found the perfect place for a church down in a beautiful valley close to the river. In fact, the spot was so perfect that he couldn't stop thinking about it. When he got back home to Wisconsin, he wrote a poem about this idyllic spot and his imagined church and later set it to music. The title was "Church in the Wildwood." As some writers do, Pitts put it in a drawer and forgot about it.

In the meantime, the residents of Bradford grew tired of meeting for worship services in various places in the town and decided to build a church. Time and materials were donated, and by 1862 the building was enclosed and not a penny spent. However, it still needed to be painted. The cheapest paint at the time was Ohio Mineral Paint, which would protect the wood but unfortunately came only in brown. By 1864, the building was finished.

During this time, Pitts had married. He and his wife lived in Wisconsin until 1862, when the couple moved to Fredericksburg to be near his wife's elderly parents. Pitts was hired to teach singing classes at the Bradford Academy. He once took a walk to what was once the empty lot surrounded by wildwoods, and there stood a little brown church, just as he had written about those many years ago!

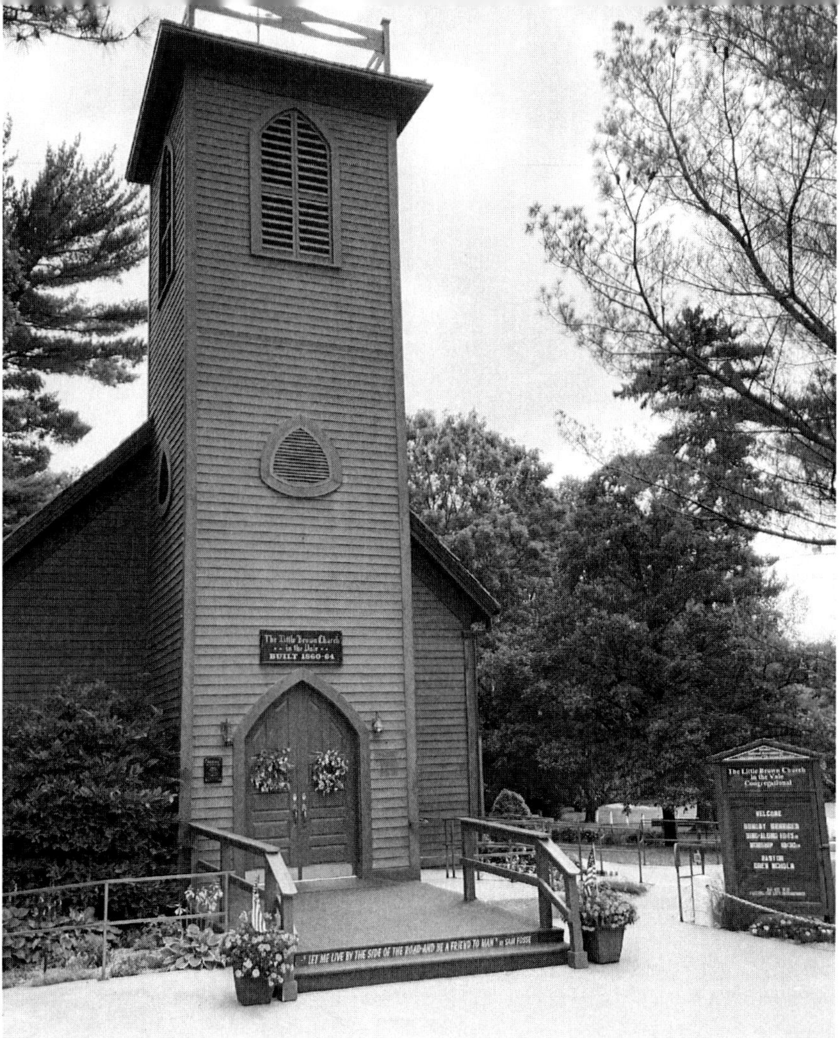

The Little Brown Church in Nashua is also the subject of the song "Church in The Wildwood."

He found his song and taught it to his music students, who later sang it at the church's dedication in 1864. And so there it was—a song that had been written about a church that wasn't there, and a church, built as described, by people with no knowledge of the song.

Today, thousands of people have been married in the Little Brown Church, and odds are good that William Pitts's song has been sung at most of those weddings.

Welcome Back, Paddlefish!

After 100 years, a native species of fish will be returning to Okoboji. The paddlefish, one of the most primitive of fish, can be distinguished by its elongated paddle-like snout, long gill covers, and shark-like body, according to the Iowa Department of Natural Resources (DNR). Formerly abundant in the Mississippi Valley area, it was overly exploited and experienced decline because of environmental concerns, so it is no longer common except in certain places along the river.

Its large size and bizarre shape have made paddlefish interesting to anglers and others. For those who want bragging rights to the biggest fish caught, paddlefish over six feet long have been taken from Iowa. They are long-lived fish, surviving up to 20 or even 30 years. When young, paddlefish have tiny, fine teeth, but as they age they lose their teeth. They exist on a diet of plankton and small plants.

The last recorded catch of a paddlefish on the Iowa Great Lakes was in 1919. It was the largest ever caught in Okoboji, weighing in at 210 pounds and six and a half feet long. In fact, the Iowa Great Lakes Maritime Museum holds a replica of that fish. Records of this mammoth fish began in 1900 in Okoboji and ended in 1919.

Paddlefish are a river fish that came into the Okoboji Lakes from the Missouri River by way of the Little Sioux River, and the reason they died out was a dam. Around 1900, a dam was constructed at the outlet of Lower Gar Lake, so the paddlefish could no longer make their way into the Okoboji Lakes.

So where are the paddlefish coming from after having disappeared for over 100 years? They're being raised at the Rathbun State Fish Hatchery

The primitive-looking paddlefish may appear alarming but is toothless when it reaches maturity. Courtesy of Iowa Department of Natural Resources

and will be making their way to Okoboji as soon as water temperatures are cool enough for safe transport. A fisheries biologist from the DNR, Mike Hawkins, says restocking paddlefish in the Great Lakes will need to be done on a regular basis. The reason is that paddlefish aren't lake reproducers, but more river reproducers. The recovery and restocking work being done with paddlefish "is a great success story for the species that is really a living fossil."

West Lake Okoboji is now home to another fish species, the paddlefish.

Coffin-Making Monks

Located in the fertile farmlands and rugged woods of eastern Iowa around Peosta and Dubuque is the New Melleray Abbey, founded in 1849 by Irish monks from Mount Melleray, Ireland. Trappist monks live and work in this beautiful part of the state, following the centuries-old Rule of St. Benedict. Embracing silence and separation from the dominant culture, they follow a life of contemplative prayer, reading, and work.

Being mindful of God throughout the day includes being mindful at work, and the monks believe in supporting themselves instead of relying on donations. Their business, Trappist Caskets (which is located directly across the road from the monastery), opened in 1999 and provides their principal means of self-support. The monks not only provide grieving families with support at the time they need it most, but they also view their woodworking as cooperating with God's creation. The physical exercise that this manual labor provides is a complement to their study and prayer.

Being stewards of the land, the monks have taken great care to grow and maintain their own forests, which provide over a third of all the wood they use in their caskets and urns. With the exception of their simple pine caskets, all are made from classic hardwoods, adding to their beauty and strength. Approximately 1,900 caskets are sold or given away annually, and since the business has grown and the number of monks hasn't kept up, laypeople are now working alongside the monks from New Melleray.

A unique ministry offered through Trappist Caskets concerns families who have lost a child. Caskets are offered in compassion and faith at no cost to them. This service is an expression of the monks' prayer for all children to be commended to God's love and care forever.

Making (and selling) coffins ties in with the Trappist Monks' mission at the New Melleray Abbey: "Pray and work." Courtesy of Becky Elsbernd

Guests are welcome to tour not only the monastery, but also the business where Trappist Caskets is located. The production facility has enormous storage racks six caskets tall, and the monks work to keep those racks full at all times. A humbling thought is that these racks are full of what will be the final "home" for individuals awaiting them.

Visiting this place will provide a different perspective on life, silence, mindfulness, and death. The mission of Trappists Caskets can be summed up in three Latin words: *ora et labora* . . . or "pray and work." This has served the Trappist monks well for centuries and will continue for many more.

Iowa's Only Island City

Looking for an island getaway? In Iowa? Only an hour away from the Quad Cities, Sabula is a quaint little town nestled right on the Mississippi River between Clinton and Bellevue. And yes, it's Iowa's only island city.

It wasn't always an island, however. It was physically connected to Iowa until 1939, when a lock and dam was built between Clinton, Iowa, and Fulton, Illinois. Sabula was then "cut off" because the dam permanently submerged the lowland area to the west of the town. Talk about instant status—from a regular town to an island city!

Sabula residents have beautiful views day and night.

Sabula had an interesting history even before that, however. The first European settler arrived in Sabula on a log. Isaac Dorman crossed the Mississippi from Illinois on a log and decided to settle on this town site, along with several Native American families who continued to live there when other settlers came. A disagreement about what to name the town finally ended with "Sabula," which was close enough to the suggested Latin word *sabulum* for sand but "more elegant and easier to pronounce." This fits perfectly, as the town has very sandy soil.

In the early days, a button factory and hog slaughterhouses were some of the town's industries. Clams were abundant, so the clam shells were made into pearl buttons, and the meat from the clams was fed to the hogs. The town took advantage of its natural resources and thrived until the invention of the plastic button, which shut the pearl button factory down. No hog farms are on the island anymore, although hog farming is still a huge industry in Iowa.

At one mile long and a quarter mile wide, Sabula houses around 500 residents, most commuting to nearby towns in Iowa or Illinois for work. However, this unique little town offers all the amenities of any other small town. A school, bank, public library, and bed & breakfast, along with restaurants, bars, and even a convenience store, are among the businesses keeping the town running.

For tourists looking for something a little off the beaten path, Sabula has a great beach and marina and offers fishing, boating, hunting, and camping for the adventurers. How often can you spend a night on a floating cottage or in a houseboat?

If nothing else, Sabula can let you brag that you visited an island city . . . in Iowa.

Crossing State Lines for Candy

Picture yourself as the owner of a candy company. It's the early 1920s, and candy bars are becoming more popular. In fact, they're so popular that grocery stores can barely keep them in stock. Nearly 40,000 candy bars have been invented so far, and you want a "piece of the pie." What do you do? If you're the Palmer Candy Company, you invent, produce, and sell the Bing candy bar!

There is nothing more beautiful than the sight of a delicious Twin Bing. Courtesy Wikimedia Commons

The Bing was born in 1923 and consisted of chocolate and roasted peanuts combined with nougat and wrapped around a cherry center. It was a bit of heaven, and people couldn't get enough of it. Originally, it came in four different flavors–maple, vanilla, pineapple, and cherry, but the cherry was everyone's favorite by far.

Today, the Bing candy bar is still produced by hand and remains a Midwest favorite. Of all the chocolates and confections the company has developed over the years, the Bing still remains "the bomb!"

Before the Bing, the Palmer Candy Company had a long history beginning in 1878, when a fire destroyed the home of Edward Cook (E. C.) Palmer in St. Joseph, Michigan. He packed up his family and moved to Sioux City, where he bought a wholesale grocery operation. In 1892, his son opened a wholesale fruit company with his dad and brother, forming Palmer and Company.

This company got into the candy business in 1900 and moved into a new four-story building with up-to-date technologies such as ammonia cold storage and their own electric generator. They soon became well known for making delicious, hand-dipped boxed chocolates and penny candy among other confections. And then came 1923 and the Bing . . . and they never looked back!

Bing candy bars were originally sold individually, but in the 1960s inflation threatened to increase the price of a Bing bar, so Palmer Candy Company decided to offer "more Bing for the buck." Each package was changed to contain two large humps—or two "bings"—and the "Twin Bing" was born in 1973. (And of course, three bumps are even better than two, so in 1986, the "King Bing" hit the market.)

The candy bar "worth crossing state lines for" has been made by hand in Sioux City, Iowa, for over 100 years in a five-generation family-owned and operated company. As Marty Palmer, president and CEO of the Palmer Candy Company says, "It is something really special!"

For Bing lovers, a Twin Bing is good, but a King Bing reigns supreme.

Glow-in-the-Dark Trail

What glows green at night, is two miles long, and attracts people from all over? It's Nathan's Miles Glow Trail in Vinton, the longest glow-in-the-dark trail in the US!

This glow trail with the nickname of Nathan Smiles is named for Nathan Hesson, former Vinton City Council member and advocate of the project, who died in January 2021. Hesson wanted his hometown to have the world's longest glow-in-the-dark trail. Unfortunately, he never got to see it come to life, as he passed away four months before it was finished.

The city of Vinton was making plans for a three-mile loop around the school campus, and the addition of glow-in-the-dark stones to the surface was an idea that was incorporated right before its construction. Two miles of this three-mile loop contain 3,000 pounds of emerald -green, half-inch glow stones, which were chosen because of their brightness. The glow stones run on solar power, and only 15 minutes of charge time can light the path for 15 hours. The glow stones come from a manufacturer in Canada and are completely non-toxic and non-radioactive.

This unique trail draws visitors to the area, and residents of Vinton now have a fun trail to walk or ride on, day or night. The trailhead starts at the corner of 21st Street and Second Avenue, on the northeast side of the school, and is open 24 hours a day. Nathan's Miles connects to an existing sidewalk trail and will soon be joined to another path to make a five-kilometer loop.

This beautiful memorial to the former council member known for his ready smile and dedication to his community is an appropriate one, as Hesson was an outdoor enthusiast and champion for his hometown. His struggle with Loeys-Dietz syndrome over the years caused him to slow down, but he never lost sight of his dream of using the completed trail with his children one day. What a legacy Hesson left, not only for his family but also for the Vinton residents and visitors who can spend healthy family time on the trail.

It's never too dark to exercise on this trail. Courtesy of Traveliowa.com

A Miracle in Stone

The Grotto in West Bend has been described as "a miracle in stone" and is sometimes called "The Eighth Wonder of the World." A composite of nine separate grottos that each depict a scene in the life of Christ, this geological wonder is on the National Register of Historic Places and has been featured in *Roadside America* and the movie *The Straight Story*.

The man behind the grotto was a young seminarian, Father Paul Matthias Dobberstein, who was critically ill with pneumonia. He prayed to the Blessed Virgin Mary to help him regain his health and promised to build a shrine in her honor if he lived. His illness passed, and he came to West Bend in 1898 as a pastor. He began working on keeping his promise in 1912, as he had been stockpiling rocks and precious stones for a decade.

Father Dobberstein worked continuously on the project over the next four decades until his death in 1954. In the summertime he worked outside, placing stones by hand, while in the winter he worked indoors, setting stones, minerals, and shells into large sections of concrete. He also traveled the world in the spring and fall in search of new materials for his expanding shrine. Overall, he traveled over 800,000 miles in his hunt for unique rocks and minerals.

Matt Szerensce worked with Father Dobberstein as a full-time collaborator for 52 years, starting right after he graduated from high school. The Grotto became his life's work as well. Father Dobberstein was 74 years old when Father Louis Greving was sent to take over his clerical duties and assist with the ongoing building project. These three men are responsible for the Grotto of the Redemption finally being completed 100 years after construction on it began.

The Grotto of the Redemption is now known as the largest man-made grotto in the world and is also home to one of the largest collections of precious stones and gems found in one place, their worth estimated at $4.3 million.

Over 100,000 people visit the Grotto each year to marvel at the impressive sight, which takes up over a metropolitan city block. At one time it even caught the eye of Walt Disney, who wanted to replicate it for Disneyland. However, engineering experts told him the structure was a "once in a lifetime" piece that simply could not be matched.

The Grotto is home to one of the largest collections of precious stones and gems found in one place.

Inside the "haunted" Roseman Covered Bridge near Winterset.

Chapter Four

Dark Tales

Not everything is as it seems, and Iowa has its share of stories that will give you the creeps. Some of the frightening or sad tales included here are very much historically accurate, such as stories of massacres, plane crashes, and unexplained deaths. Others are considered more folklore or myths that keep people guessing.

A covered bridge that became famous in a novel (and later a movie) is also known as a haunted area. Several old, abandoned buildings allow people's imaginations to get the best of them . . . or witness things only seen in scary movies. And then there are the ghosts, such as the theater ghosts who still seek the limelight and the candy-loving ones who come out only at midnight.

What would a state be without the stories of one monster or another? Just like the age-old discussion about the existence of Bigfoot or Sasquatch, one Iowa town still celebrates the sighting of an unwanted visitor many years ago.

And some dark tales are heartbreaking because they really happened, and the state pulls together to remember and honor the loved ones who were lost.

Survivor of the Spirit Lake Massacre

One of Iowa's extremely harsh winters caused a food shortage so serious that both European-American settlements and Indigenous encampments were threatened with starvation. One of these camps included the Wahpekute leader Inkpaduta and his followers.

To provide a brief background, the Dakota Indian nation for years had lived as hunter-gatherers in what is now the Arnolds Park area. New settlers got along peacefully with them for the most part until the two groups had to compete for land and resources, and the scarcity caused by a harsh winter exacerbated tensions. The conflict turned violent in what would become known as the Spirit Lake Massacre.

Here's how it happened: With his tribe on the verge of starvation, Inkpaduta tried to barter with the settlers for food but was refused. Tension ran high, and anger turned into violence. Fighting began on March 8, 1857, and over the next six days, 33 settlers were killed, including 13-year-old Abbie Gardner's parents and brother. An unknown number of Dakota were also killed.

Gardner's family was brutally murdered right in front of her. In her words: "I was dragged from the never-to-be-forgotten scene. No language can ever suggest, much less adequately portray, my feelings as I passed that door." She was taken captive, along with three other women, and the tribe fled north to Minnesota.

From Minnesota the tribe went west to the Dakotas, killing two of their four captives. Abbie was one of two to survive, and almost three months later she was released with the other woman after a ransom (consisting of horses, blankets, and provisions) was paid.

After her release, she went to live in Hampton with her sister (who fortunately was out of the family cabin during their massacre). She met and married Cassville Sharp later that year, and together they raised two children before separating sometime in the mid-1880s. She supported herself by giving speeches about her time in captivity and went on to write a book about her experience.

She returned to Arnolds Park in 1891, bought her family's cabin, and operated it as one of Iowa's first tourist attractions until her death in 1921.

The Gardner family cabin is the site of the 1857 Spirit Lake Massacre where 13-year-old Abbie Gardner's family was killed. Courtesy of Carol Dettmer

Axe Murder House

A well-loved family attended a church service together one warm summer evening in Villisca. They went home, along with two of their children's friends who were spending the night. In the morning all eight of them were dead . . . all murdered in their sleep, each bludgeoned by an axe.

The family included Josiah Moore, the father; his wife, Sarah; their four children, Herman, Mary, Arthur, and Paul; and their children's friends, Lena and Ina Stillinger. The six children were all under the age of 12. Someone had come into the house during the evening and committed an unbelievably grisly murder.

The bodies were discovered the following morning when a neighbor became concerned and contacted Josiah's brother. What he found was beyond shocking. Besides the bodies, the murder weapon (the axe) was in the same room as the two Stillinger girls.

The authorities chased multiple leads over the years, including Reverend Lyn George Jacklin Kelly, who left Villisca on a train that morning and told fellow passengers about eight dead souls in Villisca who were butchered in their beds. The bodies had not yet been discovered at that point.

Months later, Kelly confessed and said that God had whispered to him "to suffer the children to come to me." He recanted his confession during his trial and was acquitted. No one else has been tried for the murders.

The "Axe Murder House" had various occupants in the following years. Every resident had something unusually upsetting occur—enough to send them moving out as quickly as possible. In the 1990s, the home was bought and restored by historians Martha and Gavin Linn, who seemed to turn back time, getting the house to look exactly as it did on the night of the crime. Today, the Josiah B. Moore house is on the National Register of Historic Places.

The Linns never intended to live in this house. Instead, they thought it might make a good true crime tourist attraction. What they hadn't expected was the large market of ghost-hunters who flocked to visit the house, night and day, even choosing to stay overnight in the murder rooms.

The house was sold in 2023 to US Ghost Adventures, a ghost tour company that offers spooky and haunted experiences in over 100 cities. Tours and overnight stays are still available . . . if you dare.

Also known as the Josiah B. and Sara Moore House, the Villisca "Axe Murder House" is on the National Register of Historic Places. Courtesy of Wikimedia Commons; Jason McLaren, photographer

A Tale of Two (Haunted) Bridges

Banwell (Terror) Bridge

Just outside of Fort Dodge lies a bridge with an interesting and eerie background. The Banwell Bridge, also known as the Terror Bridge (or sometimes even "Tara" Bridge, as it used to be close to the town of Tara) has a history dating back to the 1800s.

Ranking at number 13 on Travel Iowa's "13 of Iowa's Most Haunted" list, the Banwell Bridge has many stories surrounding it. Perhaps the most sad and gruesome one involves a woman and her three children.

It is said that a woman brought her three children to this bridge to watch the trains pass underneath. Instead of a pleasant time watching the train, she threw each child off the bridge as the train approached, killing them instantly. She then jumped off the bridge herself and died.

Fort Dodge locals warn against going on this bridge at all at night. But if it's absolutely necessary, they advise you not to stop your car on the bridge without locking your doors and windows "as the woman's spirit might try to throw you off." Brave visitors who actually exit their

The Banwell (Terror) Bridge has some sad and spooky tales in its past.

cars have reported seeing "strange orbs" or hearing voices in the woods. Sometimes a woman's moans beneath the bridge have been heard, and even more strange than that, visitors have discovered handprints on their cars after they have left the bridge.

A chocolate-loving ghost is what visitors may run into at midnight on the Rainbow Bridge in Lake City. Courtesy of Wikimedia Commons

Rainbow Bridge

If the Banwell (Terror) Bridge isn't your thing, maybe something more light-hearted and kitschy might appeal to you. The Rainbow Bridge in Lake City is just the spot.

Nicknamed the "rainbow" bridge because of its arched profile (and not for the colorful graffiti covering it now), the bridge is also known as the Marsh Rainbow Arch Bridge.

People claim that this bridge is also haunted. But this ghost has more of a sense of humor . . . and a sweet tooth. Supposedly, this ghost is a chocoholic, and if you place an unopened bar of chocolate in the middle of the bridge at midnight and leave, the chocolate will be gone in five minutes, with the wrapper intact.

Two haunted bridges in the same state; one sinister, one sweet. There's something for everyone in Iowa.

Beware of the Black Angel

Ask anyone in Iowa City if you should venture out on a solo visit to the Black Angel statue in Oakland Cemetery after dark, and the answer will almost always be a resounding "Never!" This statue's history is both sad and spooky, probably two factors that made it appear on the "Top 11 Haunts Along the Lincoln Heritage Byway" on the Prairie Rivers of Iowa website.

The history of the eight-and-a-half-foot-tall statue is quite a story in itself. It was commissioned by Bohemian immigrant Teresa Dolezal Feldevert, a practicing physician who came to Iowa with her young son, Eddie, to be a midwife. Sadly, he died of meningitis at the age of 18, and Teresa buried him in Oakland Cemetery in 1891, with a tree-stump monument as his headstone. When she later buried her husband, Nicholas Feldevert, in 1911, she hired Bohemian artist Mario Kobel to design and craft a $5,000 monument to honor her son and husband—and someday, herself.

Located in Iowa City's Oakland Cemetery, this Black Angel statue is hauntingly beautiful and holds years of mysteries.

Disagreements about what came next make it hard to know what really happened. The statue was either installed upon its completion in 1918 or was held for years in a barn before installation at that time. The outcome didn't satisfy Teresa, and she refused to pay the $5,000, also taking Kobel to court. She eventually lost the case and died several years later in 1924. Teresa was laid to rest with her family underneath the statue, even though her date of death was never added to the statue's inscription.

The first thing a person might notice about the statue besides the color itself is that the angel is looking downward instead of upward. Many angels are depicted with heads and wings uplifted "to symbolize the soul's ascent into heaven." The Black Angel statue is just the reverse, so that it looks as if she is carrying the weight of the world on her back.

And the color? Why has the statue turned black? So many theories exist regarding the reason, but there is a scientific explanation. The bronze statue has experienced oxidation over the years, turning it black.

Myths about the Black Angel

Most of the myths have something to do with kissing and death, in that order. Believe them or not, the Black Angel is a curiosity to behold.

Anyone who kisses the Angel will die immediately.

If you kiss someone in front of the Angel at midnight on Halloween, you will die within seven years.

Touching the Angel at midnight on Halloween means death within seven years.

Every passing Halloween causes the Angel to turn one shade darker as a reminder of the people she has killed.

The Brady Street Banshee

Loud screams, whistling, and sounds of a banshee are what you might hear on Brady Street in Davenport. What's a banshee? If you have Irish ancestors, you may be familiar with the saying, "Stop howling like a banshee." In Irish lore, a banshee is "a female spirit whose wailing warns of an impending death in a house." It's definitely not a sound you'd want to hear in any case.

It's also a sound one family must have heard four times within the first year they moved to Brady Street back around 1918. Four members in the Schachts family . . . and four deaths. The young son fell out of an upstairs window and impaled himself on a fence; the daughter drowned in the bathtub; the mother hung herself in the basement; and the father followed her lead (but in the kitchen). Bad luck, to say the least, seemed to be rampant in this home.

After a few years with the house sitting empty (because who would want to buy a cursed home?) the price went down, and a Mafia member found it to be a great deal. A few of his "lady friends" moved in, and all of a sudden it became known as a brothel as well as a hideout for some Chicago gangsters. It's even rumored that Al Capone spent some time here!

Hearing the terrible howl of a banshee supposedly signifies something awful is about to happen. Courtesy of Wikimedia Commons

After ghosts began to appear, including one with an especially loud wail whom they named the "Brady Street Banshee," the house quickly emptied. Next up for residents? College students who needed apartments. Between strange noises (including what sounded like moaning), cold drafts, and covers being ripped off the bed in the middle of the night, the college students didn't stay there long. The house again became vacant and soon was torn down and replaced with a parking lot.

What happened to the banshee? Legend has it that it moved from house to house on Brady Street. Do residents of this neighborhood still hear the *awful* wailing? It's a mystery, and one that may remain unanswered.

However, the Davenport Public Library did some additional research once it was discovered that the original location of the Brady Street Banshee was only blocks away from the library itself. They found no historical evidence of the Schachts family on that street or during that time period.

So is the Brady Street Banshee fact or fiction? It seems no one who heard it is around anymore.

Brady Street, late 1900s. Courtesy of Wikimedia Commons

Vaudeville Ghosts in Cresco

The Cresco Opera House—for all its architectural beauty and its history spanning over 100 years—is also a little bit haunted. Once a home for vaudeville shows, it is now a home for live performances as well as movies. Apparently, this theater also harbors other things unseen. Legend says old vaudeville performers still want their stage time, continuing to haunt the place they once thought would make them big stars. People have witnessed some of the "performances" of these vaudeville ghosts on stage.

Not every spooky performance happens under the lights, though. Live performers have looked out from the stage and spotted a lone viewer sitting there. He never buys a ticket, and he disappears before anyone can approach him.

Some actors don't let a little thing like death make them leave the limelight. Courtesy of crescotheatreoperahouse.com

Upstairs in the costume shop is another popular place for ghost-spotting. A Cresco newspaper included a great anecdote about this. A woman who was very active in theater productions said she and a friend were on the second floor where all the costumes were stored. Between the rows of costumes they saw a lady in a colonial dress, walking from one rack to another. The two women thought the lady might be the theater's costumer, but as they walked across the room, they found no one there.

Similar reports of strange things happening at the concession stand and the basement have been shared. Doors opening and closing on their own, unusual sounds when no one should be inside the building, strange electrical disturbances . . . all of these are a paranormal lover's delight.

But all of this is classic theater lore, right? When a theater/opera house has been in existence as long as Cresco's has, the stories are bound to be good ones. And theater ghosts don't seem to be very harmful. They just want to share the limelight . . . because once an actor, always an actor!

Hauntings Are Grand in Dubuque

Stories of the paranormal are common in Dubuque's Grand Opera House. Most spirits in the building are known as "Sarah," who was a young woman who may have died here in the early 1900s after being left by her lover. Shadowy apparitions of women can be seen in the costume shop, too.

The basement has spirits who seem to be pranksters, sliding things out of people's pockets and moving around items that have been left there. Maybe we all have an ancestor of this spirit in our own basements . . .

Lake of the Dead Man

With a name like "Dead Man's Lake," it has to have a great story. Located in one of Iowa's oldest state parks, Pilot Knob, this lake is a four-acre floating sphagnum bog hidden within the park and home to many unique wildlife species. The bog is the only one of its kind in Iowa. Since the lake is highly acidic, only a few specially adapted species can survive there.

One of those is a carnivorous plant. Before you go thinking about Audrey II in the musical *Little Shop of Horrors*, pull your expectations back a bit. This lake supports the round-leaved sun dew, which is a small plant that attracts, catches, and eats insects. It's widespread in the world, but pretty rare in Iowa. It's a low-grower and requires a very moist, acidic environment, which is exactly what this bog offers.

If you were to set foot in the bog, it might feel "like you're walking on an extra soft bed." And something like a child's urge to jump up and down on a bed might come over you in the middle of a bog. Your jumping might cause your feet to get wet, but if you walked a bit to either side you might encounter a dry spot. Becoming overly confident, you move again . . . and sink a bit further than you had earlier. So a bog isn't necessarily deep, but you just never know what you're getting into.

As to the name of the lake, different stories surround it. One is that an early pioneer who was passing by led his oxen out on the ice to let them drink. The ice gave way, and "the oxen, wagon, and man sank to a spongy coffin."

The most authentic story has to do with a lone Native American who lived by the lake. Apparently, he had a falling out with his other tribe members and chose to live alone by the lake. Upon his death he was buried in a nearby cave, and the entrance was sealed.

Another version of that story includes the same solitary Native American telling a pioneer that the name of the lake was the "Lake of the Dead Man," because "he was dead so far as his tribe was concerned."

Nearly half of Dead Man's Lake in Pilot Knob State Park is composed of a floating sphagnum bog. Several tales surround the name of this interesting body of water. Courtesy of Helen Goodrich

Hidden Haunted Building

Who knew that one of the most haunted buildings in the entire United States is hidden in the middle of 11 acres of cornfields right here in Iowa? The Edinburgh Manor in Scotch Grove began as a county poor farm.

A poor farm (or poorhouse) was run by the government and offered housing and food to the poor in exchange for labor in the home or fields. The house held not only the needy but also some who were incurably insane, disabled, or elderly and abandoned by their families. Edinburgh was host to many residents, also known as "inmates," over the years. Some passed through and moved on to other places; others died on the farm.

Foreboding on the outside, Edinburgh Manor even spooks paranormal investigators. Courtesy of Edinburgh Manor

Poor farms were no longer needed after the Social Security Act became law in 1935 and were either torn down or abandoned by the 1950s. That being the case, the original farm building in Scotch Grove was demolished in 1910, and an entirely new facility opened in 1911, the current Edinburgh Manor. An imposing 12,000-square-foot, two-story building, the Manor was home to both men and women.

During the 2000s, the cost of taking care of the residents became prohibitive, and they were moved to a nearby facility in Anamosa. The Manor closed in 2010. When the last employees and residents left the building, they walked out the door and left everything as it was. Many documents and personal belongings can still be found there.

New owners bought the Manor to preserve its history. However, after a number of unexplained events, they decided to open it up for visitors and paranormal investigations. Some of the reports of paranormal occurrences include stories of spirits that giggle in the dark, scratch people's faces, and actually knock people down.

Numerous events have happened on each floor, but the basement is home to the spirit known as "The Joker" because of his malevolent nature. Most often "felt" in the small, formerly padded room, the Joker has thrown dishes to the floor, had screaming fits, and given people the overwhelming sense of an evil presence. It's best not to linger too long, as the Joker doesn't seem to like entertaining visitors.

Take a tour through the Manor—or stay overnight—and walk into rooms that feel frozen in time, with toys scattered and table settings ready for dinner. Every room offers a chance meeting with a spirit, night or day.

Once a celebrated new school for the Washington Consolidated School District, the Farrar Schoolhouse is a known haunted location in Iowa.

School's in Session . . . for the Brave!

At one time, the Farrar Schoolhouse was a modern, beautiful facility built specifically to merge the area's one-room country schoolhouses and create the Washington Township Consolidated School District. The year was 1919, and C. G. Geddes donated six acres of his farm to accommodate this new school, which included a stage, an auditorium, boiler heating, electric lights, and indoor bathrooms. Hundreds of citizens from miles around came to celebrate at the dedication ceremony on April 1, 1922. An orchestra played on the stage, and a banquet was served to all in attendance.

Not everyone was pleased, however. Some were unhappy with the $100,000 price tag, and one man refused to come to the celebration, calling it a "monument to the arrogance and vanity of the school board."

Once again, in 2002, hundreds of people gathered in the schoolhouse where a band played and a banquet was served. This was a more somber occasion, however, as it marked the 80-year-old schoolhouse closing its doors for the last time.

After the school sat abandoned for nearly five years, Jim and Nancy Oliver bought the building in 2006. The Olivers made the building their home while they slowly worked to restore it to its original appearance. But they soon found out they were not in the schoolhouse alone . . .

They discovered what decades of school employees and students already knew: the school was haunted. Over the years, students and employees heard mysterious voices and doors slamming, and they saw unnatural, shadowy figures walking the hallways and stairwells and then suddenly vanishing.

The Olivers had their own paranormal experiences as well. One time, Nancy became unsteady on some stairs and felt a steady hand on her shoulder, helping her regain her balance. She turned to thank her husband for the help only to find that no one was there! Many other weird and unexplained experiences happened to the couple and others who visited the schoolhouse.

Since 2007, the Farrar schoolhouse has seen many guests interested in exploring the paranormal side of the building. An international psychic first confirmed the Olivers' suspicions, and many others soon followed. Psychics, paranormal experts, and the Discovery Channel's *My Ghost Story* and *Ghost Stalkers* are but a few of them.

Perhaps the spirits couldn't get enough of their favorite schoolhouse. One thing is certain: school is never out for the summer here. In July 2024, YouTubers Sam Golback and Colby Brock purchased the Farrar Elementary School and filmed their experience living there for a week. The mysteries of this haunted location live on.

Romantic Covered Bridge Has a Dark Side

If you recognize this bridge, maybe it's because you either read Robert James Waller's book or saw the movie version of *Bridges of Madison County*. Fans also know it as "Francesca's bridge," as it was where Francesca left a note inviting Robert to dinner. The movie starred Meryl Streep and Clint Eastwood, and the bridges in the movie are very much real. The six covered bridges are picturesque and ooze Iowa charm. However, one of the bridges has a darker side.

The Roseman Covered Bridge, built in 1883 by Harvey P. Jones and George K. Foster, originally cost $2,930. It is 104 feet long with a flat roof and still sits in its original location. In 1992 it was renovated at a cost of $152,515, some of which was provided by a federal restoration grant. (That's not the dark side, but it is crazy inflation over the years!)

This bridge gained fame for being "haunted" in 1892. A prisoner escaped from the county jail, and the sheriff formed a posse, chasing the man to the Roseman Bridge. The convict entered the bridge, and

the sheriff had his men split up on either side of the bridge to trap him. Apparently, in the confusion, some shots were fired, injuring some of the members of the posse. The convict let out a terrible scream, and then he disappeared as if he vanished into thin air.

Since that incident, other strange things have happened around the bridge. Visitors have claimed to hear laughter or they have felt a cold spot in the middle of the bridge. People have also reported unusual experiences while walking their dogs across the Roseman Covered Bridge. Their dogs have become frightened and have refused to continue crossing the bridge—or if they do, the hair on their dog's back stands up while walking across.

Other reports include people seeing full-body apparitions, hearing voices, and even feeling the bridge shake. When Central Iowa Paranormal Investigators visited the bridge, they had their own unexplained incidents. The creepiest one was when they used their recording device and it picked up an EVP (Electronic Voice Phenomenon) telling them to leave.

Whether or not you believe this bridge is haunted, the Roseman Bridge is one of Iowa's iconic attractions, with or without the laughter.

The Roseman Covered Bridge near Winterset is romantic in the movie *The Bridges of Madison County*, but it also holds a haunting past.

Miracle in a Cornfield

July 19, 1989, marks the date of the deadliest single-aircraft accident in the history of United Airlines. United Flight 232 was en route from Denver to Chicago (with a final destination of Philadelphia) when the passengers and crew heard an explosion in the tail section.

Pilot Al Haynes soon realized that the plane was experiencing catastrophic engine failure, cutting off virtually all of the hydraulic power. With assistance from an off-duty captain, Dennis Fitch (who just happened to be on the flight), Haynes and his crew were able to head to Sioux City's airport instead of their destination in Chicago.

The United Flight 232 Memorial in Sioux City, Iowa, commemorates the heroism of the flight crew who crash-landed a crippled jet airliner, bound from Denver to Philadelphia, at the airport in the western Iowa city in 1989 and those who saved 185 of the 296 passengers and crew on the ground. Courtesy of Carol M. Highsmith, Library of Congress

The plane stayed in flight for 44 more minutes, which gave airport rescue teams time to prepare on the ground. During the landing, one of the plane's wings dipped, gouging the tarmac before it ripped off. The plane broke apart into three pieces, erupted into a fireball, and tumbled end over end until it skidded to a stop in a cornfield. Rescue crews rushed to save as many people as they could, having to fight through heavy smoke and fire to get to the crash victims. Out of 284 passengers and 12 crew members, 112 people died that day, all of them passengers.

The heroic efforts of the pilot, flight crew, and first responders saved 184 people. Experts say it was a miracle that anyone survived that day. One physician told news reporters that it was the worst thing he'd ever seen in his life.

After several investigations, the cause of the accident was found to be much more than engine failure, but "a complete failure of the hydraulic system." Examination of a damaged engine rotor that turned up in an Iowa cornfield revealed a small crack in the recovered disc as a likely cause of the crash.

For survivors of this horrific crash, it changed their lives forever. Some say they still think about it every day. Pilot Al Haynes shared that "the key to the cure" is to talk about the crash. For people in Sioux City, there is a special name they have for the disaster. It will always be a "miracle in a cornfield."

The Story of a Miracle

The Mid America Museum of Aviation and Transportation is home to the most extensive account of the crash of United Flight 232. It's the story of a miracle.

According to the museum's website, an exhibit and garden to honor all involved are part of the museum, which is located on Runway 22, the old World War II closed runway that Captain Al Haynes "could see and the crew could manage to get to."

Initial touchdown area of United Flight 232. Courtesy of Wikimedia Commons

A Lazy Susan Jail

The "Squirrel Cage" was a three-story rotary jail on Pearl Street in Council Bluffs. It was one of 18 revolving ("Lazy Susan") jails built, and it was the only three-story one ever made.

The Squirrel Cage had cells shaped like pie slice wedges on a platform that rotated in a carousel fashion. The surrounding of the entire level had a single opening, allowing only one cell at a time to be accessible. It took only one man to turn the entire cell drum using a large hand crank, which was a main selling point for this unique style of jail, which would be durable and difficult to escape.

When the Squirrel Cage was complete, it looked more like a Victorian carriage house on the outside instead of a fortress-style institution. "Opening Day" was September 10, 1885, when Pottawattamie County transferred 15 prisoners from the old courthouse jail to the Squirrel Cage Jail. And that's when the adventures began.

The jail was in continuous use until 1969, and during that time four deaths occurred. Causes of prisoners' deaths included a heart attack, a three-story fall during an attempt to carve a name in the ceiling, and a hanging. An officer was shot when a gun misfired during riot training. Paranormal experts believe that these deaths could be the causes of the haunting in this jail.

Guests and residents as early as the 1900s felt that something was amiss. They heard unexplained footsteps, voices, and whispers and saw doors moving and shadowed figures. A jailer from the 1950s was so spooked after hearing footsteps on the floor when no one was around that he refused to sleep in the jail's fourth-floor apartment. He opted to sleep on the jail's second floor rather than to be so close to the unexplainable noises.

Look inside the "squirrel cage" jail cell that revolves. Courtesy of Travel Iowa

More recent reports include the feeling of being watched or followed by someone, especially on the third and fourth floors. The voice of a little girl has been heard, and numerous full-body apparitions have been seen on various occasions. Paranormal teams have investigated at different times and suggest there is enough evidence that this jail is indeed haunted.

What lies around the curve on Stony Hollow Road?

Stony Hollow Haunting

Along with the world's most crooked street, Burlington also has the most haunted road in Iowa. You're advised to think twice before visiting the latter, Stony Hollow Road.

During the day, it's much like any other rural Iowa road. There isn't much traffic, and cars can get stuck behind slow tractors . . . kind of the norm for Iowa. But at night, beware. This road was the site of a tragic death many years ago.

Legend has it that a ghost named Lucinda can show up at night. She is supposedly the spirit of a woman from the 1800s who summoned her husband to meet her at the base of a cliff overlooking Stony Hollow Road. When he didn't show up, she assumed he had run off with another woman, so she climbed to the top and jumped to her death.

In the meantime, Lucinda's husband was simply delayed due to his wagon getting stuck in the mud. When he arrived at the predetermined spot to meet his wife, he found her—not exactly the romantic tryst either one of them had in mind.

To this day, the legend of Lucinda continues. Her ghost is said to haunt this stretch of road. If you're brave enough, you can go after dark to see if she's still there. Call out her name three times, and her faint figure should appear toward the top of the cliff. If "Lucinda" leaves a rose at your feet, it reportedly means you have only 24 hours to live!

As with any other legend or scary tale, the story differs from source to source. Some say Lucinda was awaiting her fiancé to elope that evening, while others report she was awaiting her husband, who she suspected was having an affair. And as for the demise of people wanting to see her ghost, it varies between having 24 hours to live if "Lucinda" places a rose at your feet to up to 48 hours before you "meet a tragic fate."

Whichever story is the real one, this is one scary road. If Burlington's Snake Alley makes you queasy, Stony Hollow Road may just push you over the edge.

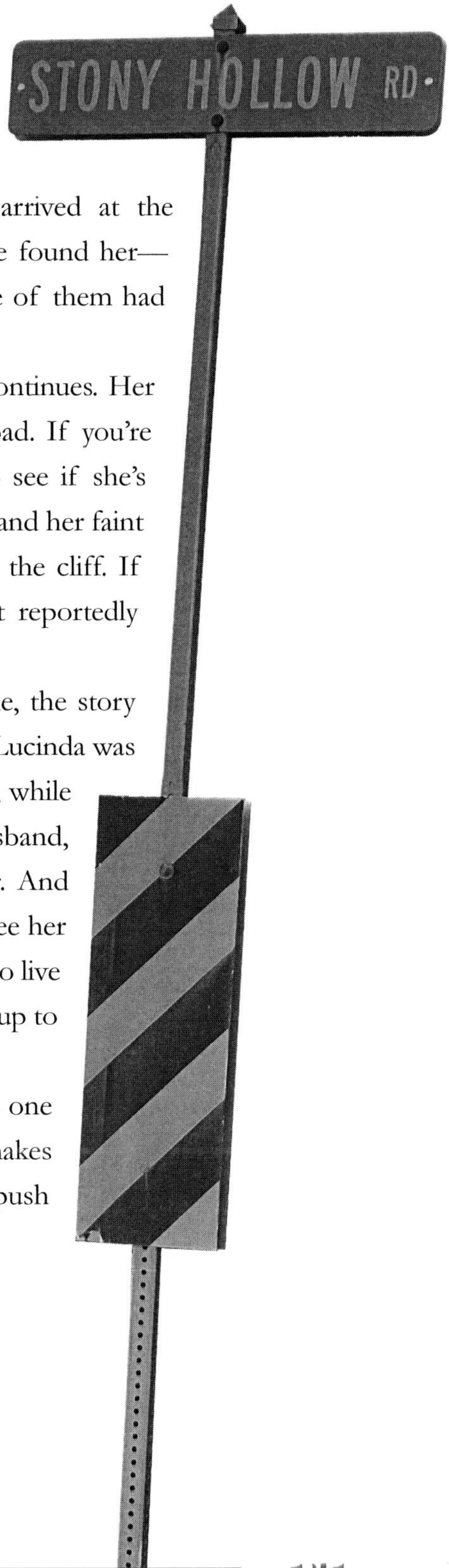

Look for the Stony Hollow sign and drive on if you dare . . .

An Unwanted Visitor

The Van Meter Visitor has inspired books, documentaries, and festivals. It has scared people in an entire town and fascinated others for over a century. Just what was it, anyway? The world may never know, but that doesn't stop people from guessing.

Here's how the "visitor" introduced itself to Van Meter back in 1903: Ulysses G. Griffith was returning home to Van Meter late one October evening when he saw a winged creature moving from rooftop to rooftop. A day later, the town's physician, Dr. Fred Alcott, was suddenly awakened by a bright light beaming in his second-story window. He got up to investigate and was shocked to find an inhuman creature standing in his doorway.

He described it later as being human-looking with wings, and he claimed to have seen a bright light coming from a horn in the creature's forehead. Although Dr. Alcott fired five shots at it from close range, the creature remained unharmed.

Over the next few days, many well-respected citizens reported seeing the same figure flying through the sky or terrorizing the town in some way after sunset. Sometimes it flew at high speeds from building to building. Sometimes it sat on top of telephone poles.

Despite so many sightings from different people, all of the reports had matching descriptions. The creature was over nine feet tall with wings, it was extremely fast, and it let off a horrific stench. And then there was that horn on its forehead that shot extremely bright lights. It was like nothing they had ever seen.

The town wasn't happy with this mysterious monster, so a group of townspeople banded together and cornered it in an abandoned coal mine. And there they saw the original creature with a miniature version of it! As witnesses described, the beasts emitted horrible noises and left behind an odor that left those in attendance stunned. The beasts seemed to fly down the shafts of the mine, and the townspeople sealed the mine forever. The "Van Meter Visitor" was never seen again.

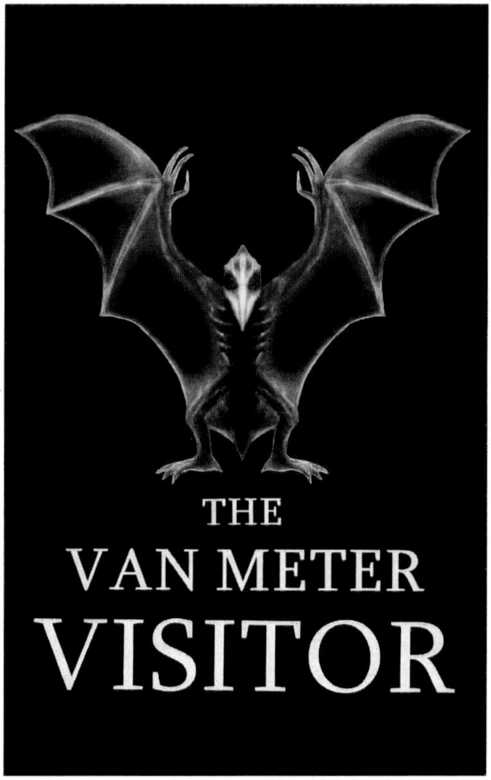

What was the Van Meter Visitor? People still gather in Van Meter annually to ponder it. Courtesy of Artwork by Kevin Lee Nelson

Just what was the creature? A bat? A dragon? To this day, it remains a cryptid, which is "an animal that has been claimed to exist but never proven to exist." So the Van Meter Visitor is in good company, with the likes of the Loch Ness Monster and Bigfoot. And the town of Van Meter remembers this creepy creature every September during a festival held in its memory.

Bikes galore and cyclists resting on the ground . . . that's RAGBRAI at the end of each day.

Chapter Five

Sports Stories

Everyone loves the story of the underdog team or athlete who rises to the top. The hard work and perseverance of an amateur on the road to becoming a legend is nothing short of spectacular and inspirational to all.

Sports stories that even a non-sports fan can enjoy are the type included in this chapter. In Iowa, people lean toward being either a Hawkeye fan or a Cyclone fan, following the University of Iowa or Iowa State University, respectively. The stadiums of these two universities are named after legendary players who have amazing stories of their own.

And then there is the Olympic gymnast; the phenomenal women's basketball star who put Iowa in the spotlight; a pro football player whose tenacity paid off; one creative man who invented the trampoline and another who developed the butterfly stroke; and the greatest bike ride of all time. All of these stories and others will make you want to go out and conquer the world . . . one stroke, jump, or step at a time.

Iowa's Man of Legends

Nile Kinnick weighed only 170 pounds and stood 5' 7" tall. His high school career consisted of winning on the football field and in the classroom. Born in Adel in 1918, Kinnick chose to attend the University of Iowa after high school as its football program at the time needed help.

His first two years were promising, and then came his junior year and an injury to his ankle. Many of his teammates thought it was broken, but no one ever found out, as Kinnick was a Christian Scientist who refused to allow his ankle to be examined. He still punted 41 times that year, averaging 41.1 yards per punt, which made him the fourth best punter in the nation.

Enter a new football coach for Iowa, Dr. Eddie Anderson, in 1939. During Iowa's first two games that season, the team scored more points than it had in the entire previous year. During most of the games, many players went the full 60 minutes, earning the team the title of "Iron Men." Nile Kinnick became the center of attention, though, as he was a phenomenal player who did it all—"just as if he were the biggest man on the field instead of the smallest."

That season was "the stuff of legends," especially for Kinnick. He won accolades, prizes, and awards, besides having a persona the public loved. This was the

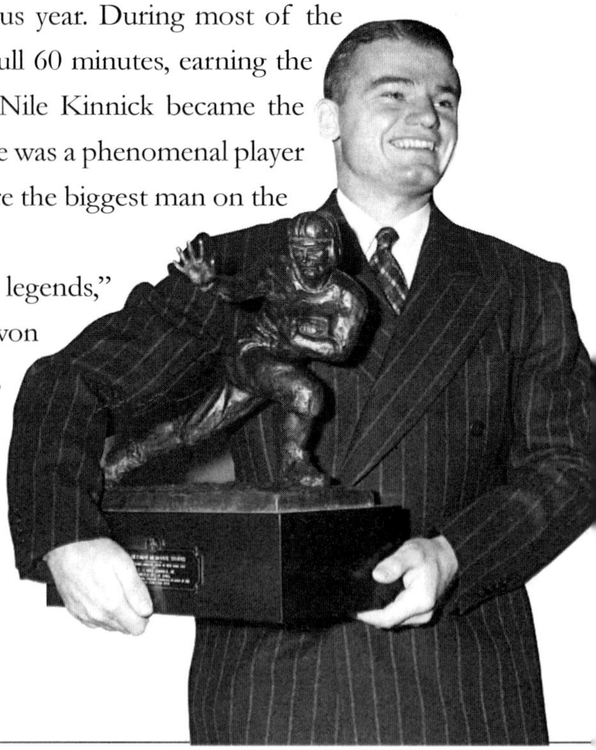

Heisman Trophy winner in 1939, Nile Kinnick was a legend on the University of Iowa football field. Courtesy of Papers of Nile Kinnick, Special Collections & Archives, The University of Iowa Libraries

magical year that Kinnick was named Big Ten MVP, and he won every player-of-the-year award, including the Heisman Trophy.

He went to law school around the time of World War II, and after completing his first year he entered the Navy to become a fighter pilot. In 1943, after his plane experienced an oil leak, he made a routine wheels-up landing on a calm sea within four miles of his carrier and in full view of other pilots. A fellow pilot saw him emerge from the cockpit, and he radioed that all seemed well. Within a minute, however, the plane sank, and the rescue party wasn't able to save him. America had lost one of its greatest All-Americans.

A bronze statue of Nile Kinnick welcomes University of Iowa fans to Kinnick Stadium, which was named in his honor.

The University of Iowa football stadium was renamed Kinnick Stadium in 1972 in honor of Kinnick, a fitting tribute to one of the greatest players ever to play on its turf. In addition, a 16-foot bronze statue of Kinnick was erected in front of the stadium in 2006. Nile Kinnick was a good example of what Iowa is all about, on and off the football field.

The Cyclone Who Did Big Things

Iowa State's first Black athlete, Jack Trice, was an Ohio native who came to Iowa State in 1922 to play football, run for the track team, and major in animal husbandry. He planned to go south after graduating to help Black farmers. The summer before his freshman year, he married Cora Mae Starland. She was 15; he was 19. They both found jobs in order to support themselves through school.

One of Trice's jobs was doing custodial work. Legend has it that he would even clean the cleats of his White teammates. Trice was reportedly very much aware of the racial attitudes of his peers. He was described as aggressive on the field and submissive off of it. Popular with fellow students and professors, he didn't seem to have many problems . . . except for the color of his skin at this time in history.

Many schools wouldn't allow a Black athlete to attend at all; some just didn't allow them to play varsity sports. When Trice arrived at Iowa State, he was one of 20 Black students on campus and the only Black athlete on the football team. Even the teams in Iowa State's own conference refused to play against any opponent with a Black player on the roster.

But the big game against Minnesota was planned for October 6, 1923, in Minneapolis, and Trice was prepared for it. He said a lengthy goodbye to Cora at their home before boarding the train to Minneapolis. When the team arrived at the Curtis Hotel, he was informed that he

Jack Trice was the first African American athlete for Iowa State College . . . and one whose life was cut short much too quickly. Courtesy of Wikimedia Commons

couldn't room or dine with his teammates—not even the night before the game when they were strategizing.

That night, Trice sat alone in his hotel room. He took out a pen and hotel stationery and wrote a letter to himself. "The honor of my race, family and self are at stake. Everyone is expecting me to do big things. I will!"

Game Day arrived, and Trice broke his collarbone on the second play. He insisted he was fine and returned to the game. During the third quarter, he was forced to the ground and trampled by University of Minnesota players and then taken to a Minneapolis hospital. He was able to make the trip home, but once again ended up in the hospital in Ames. His internal injuries warranted surgery, but the surgery itself was deemed too dangerous to perform. Jack Trice died from his injuries the following day. He was 21 years old.

Honoring Trice's Memory

In 1997, Iowa State University's football stadium was named Jack Trice Stadium to honor his memory. A statue of Trice sits at an entrance, along with an excerpt from the letter he wrote to himself, found later in one of his pockets after he died.

Recently, a new 100-ton bronze and concrete sculpture of Trice's silhouette called *Breaking Barriers* was added to the stadium, and a street was renamed Jack Trice Way in Ames. The legacy of Jack Trice lives on.

Jack Trice's statue, located on Iowa State University's central campus, honors his scholastic excellence as a student athlete.

From the Grocery Store to the Pros

Kurt Warner waves to the fans at the NFL Pro Bowl as starting quarterback for the Arizona Cardinals. Courtesy of Wikimedia Commons

Kurt Warner, who starred at quarterback for the St. Louis Rams and the Arizona Cardinals, was born in Burlington and graduated from high school in Cedar Rapids. Warner's story is just the kind of rags-to-riches tale that people love.

His parents, Gene and Sue Warner, divorced when Warner was 4 years old. His mother raised him along with his older brother, Matt. Like many single parents, she worked a number of jobs to keep them afloat. She later remarried, and the five-year marriage with the new husband wasn't exactly harmonious for her two sons.

Warner turned all of his attention to sports, excelling in basketball, baseball, and especially football, where he won state honors as a quarterback. He attended the University of Northern Iowa (UNI), redshirting his freshman year for the Panthers football team and riding the bench during the next three seasons. He thought about quitting the sport that he loved, but stuck with it, mainly due to some convincing from his parents.

He took hold of the starting position the next year and received conference honors as Offensive Player of the Year. Football wasn't all that was on his mind at this time of his life, however. He met his future wife, Brenda, a young single mother of two children, one of whom had suffered a brain injury when he was a baby. Brenda and Kurt married, and Kurt legally adopted her two children. The couple went on to have five more children in the following years.

Kurt's dream of playing for the NFL didn't seem to be in the cards, as he went undrafted following graduation. He was invited to the Green Bay Packers training camp but was cut just five weeks after the signing. Most people would have given up on their dream after this, but not Warner. He took a job back in Cedar Falls stocking shelves at the Hy-Vee grocery store for $5.50 an hour and trained in his spare time at UNI, still intent on being in the NFL someday.

Soon he was playing for the Iowa Barnstormers of the Arena Football League, and then for Amsterdam in the NFL's European league, where he finally started to turn heads. He went on to land a roster spot with the St. Louis Rams, leading them to a Super Bowl title. Warner ended his professional career at age 38 with the Arizona Cardinals. Shortly afterward, he joined the NFL Network as an analyst and was inducted into the Pro Football Hall of Fame.

From Iowa to the Silver Screen

How many people get a movie made about their story? Kurt Warner had that kind of life—the kind that Hollywood knew people could relate to. *American Underdog* starred Zachary Levi and Anna Paquin and is an inspirational account of Warner's rise from grocery-store stocker to Pro Football Hall of Famer.

American Underdog **is based on the inspirational true story of Kurt Warner who went from a stocker at a grocery store to two-time NFL MVP, Super Bowl Champion, and Hall of Fame quarterback. Fair Use, Wikipedia**

Making Swimming an Art Form

US swimmer Beulah Gundling at the Helsinki Swimming Stadium during the Helsinki Summer Olympics in 1952. Courtesy of Wikimedia Commons

When Beulah Detwiler was 14, she came home from swimming lessons embarrassed because she had nearly drowned. She vowed to do better and did what anyone hoping to perfect their technique in the pool would do . . . she went to the Cedar Rapids Public Library to check out a book on swimming written by Olympic champion and *Tarzan* actor Johnny Weissmuller. Using what she had learned, she went to the beach daily and taught herself how to float.

Fast forward to after graduation from Coe College. Although her swimming skills had greatly improved, she thought swimming laps was boring. Beulah won a half-mile race and eventually won an Iowa AAU gold medal in the backstroke. She grew tired of racing and started taking ballet lessons until one day another book changed her life. She read about rhythmic swimming and thought of a routine of swim strokes set to music, thus combining her swimming and ballet skills to create her act.

It was during this time she met her future husband, Henry Gundling, who urged her to enter a race at a water show in Minneapolis. She placed surprisingly high and started studying the sport of synchronized swimming. People may think of this as a group sport, but Beulah was a trailblazer in the solo division. It's been compared to doing a gymnastics floor routine in water.

Next stop: Canada to compete as a soloist in the Canadian Dominion Synchro Championships. She won first place with a routine she called "The Swan," which was inspired by Pavlova's "Dying Swan" ballet solo. That routine made her the first solo synchronized swimming champion in the world.

Beulah spent many more years conquering the synchronized swimming world and demonstrating the sport on four continents. She grew tired of cutthroat competitions and decided synchronized swimming should be an art form instead of an athletic competition. She and Henry founded the IAAA, International Academy of Aquatic Art, which combined water ballet, water pageantry, and synchronized swimming. They toured the world, putting on demonstrations and receiving high acclaim.

Thirty-five years after reading Johnny Weissmuller's book on how to swim, Beulah Gundling became one of the first inductees into the International Swimming Hall of Fame. Another one of those first 20 inductees was none other than . . . Johnny Weissmuller. Beulah Detwiler Gundling and her "swimming teacher" finally met!

The Caitlin Clark Effect

If there is one athlete who has brought people together, it's definitely Caitlin Clark, arguably the greatest basketball player of all time, man or woman, college and beyond. Clark is the highest-scoring athlete college basketball has ever seen. A 2024 University of Iowa graduate, Clark played for the Iowa Hawkeyes from 2020 to 2024 and is now a guard for the Indiana Fever.

Clark's former Hawkeye coach, Lisa Bluder, sang her praises: "She's the best player in America. If you go anywhere around the country where they know anything about basketball, they know who Caitlin Clark is."

If they weren't lucky game ticket holders, basketball fans (as well as people who had never watched the sport) found themselves glued to their TVs to watch any game that Clark was playing. All of a sudden, everyone had something in common to talk about: the uncanny athletic ability of a young woman from Des Moines. The NCAA made note of this phenomenon as well, saying that "Clark's generational talent brought more eyeballs to broadcasts."

Clark is definitely a must-watch performer. In fact, she was such a force on the Hawkeye court that there was a name for this: the Caitlin Clark Effect. It was a name attached to the drastic increase in game ticket sales wherever Clark was playing.

The Caitlin Clark Effect is also carrying over to her life as a pro. In a recent game, an opposing team that usually plays in a 3,500-

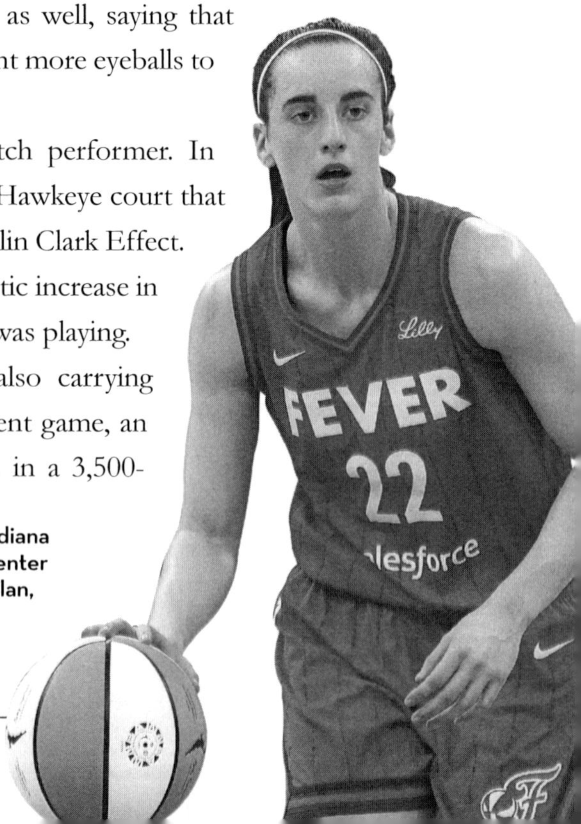

Caitlin Clark at the Minnesota Lynx vs Indiana Fever game on July 14, 2024, at Target Center in Minneapolis. Courtesy of John McClellan, Wikimedia Commons

seat arena had to move to one holding 17,000 to accommodate the fans wanting to see Clark.

Clark isn't just a phenom on the court with her amazing skills. She realizes the importance of her audience—especially young girls and women. Inspiring the next generation of female athletes is one of her passions. And she practices what she preaches, always taking time to shake hands, sign a jersey, or pose for pictures. She is walking proof of the most powerful tool we possess—our self-worth.

Caitlin Clark is a force to be reckoned with, and a person who is breaking down barriers while she breaks records. What an effect indeed!

Greatness Begins at Home

It all began at home. Clark's family in Des Moines was highly athletic, and she started playing basketball when she was five. Her dad had her join boys' teams since there were no girls' teams for her age group. Colleges started paying attention to her in middle school, and her high school games were so unbelievable that the opposing teams couldn't keep up with her. And the rest is history . . . or "her-story!"

Hawkeye fans flock around Caitlin Clark during a celebration at the Old Capitol in Iowa City for the NCAA runner-up women's basketball team. Courtesy of Joseph Murphy, Wikimedia Commons

Shawn Johnson begins her silver medal-winning floor routine in the individual all-around women's gymnastics competition at the 2008 Beijing Olympics. Courtesy of Wikimedia Commons

Life Is a Balancing Act

Parents, if your young kids are climbing cabinets and jumping off tables, you might have a future gymnast on your hands. This is what Shawn Johnson's parents noticed about her, so they enrolled her in gymnastics at age 3. When she was 6 she became one of Liang Chow's first students, and he remained her coach for almost two decades of competitive gymnastics.

And Johnson was certainly competitive. She won Olympic gold on the balance beam in 2008 in Beijing, China. Not only that, she racked up three silver medals in team, all-around, and floor exercises at the Olympics that year. Johnson made history by being just the second US gymnast to win an Olympic gold medal on the balance beam. And all this at only 16 years old!

During her internationally successful career, one might think Johnson wouldn't have had time for public school. Not so—she continued to attend West Des Moines Valley High School amidst her busy (and very public) schedule. This was due in part to her coach.

Coach Chow had been taken away from his family when he was 3, put into the Olympic system, and raised to be an Olympic gymnast in China. He very much lost his childhood and was traumatized by his upbringing. When he was 21, he decided to come to the US to open a gym where he could train Olympians while still allowing them to be children—something that he had missed out on in his life.

Somehow, he ended up in West Des Moines, and somehow, he ended up coaching this future Olympian. Johnson said that she feels blessed by how her coach treated his students. He demanded that they did "normal" kid things, like going to school and having fun. Johnson is proof that intense training in conjunction with a "normal life" can indeed yield great results.

After the 2008 Olympics, Johnson took a two-year hiatus from competitive gymnastics. She returned in 2010 to train for the 2012 Olympics but withdrew because of an injury and retired from the sport. From climbing on entertainment centers as a wild 2-year-old who "cracked her head open a lot" to making her dreams come true as an Olympic champion, Johnson had just the right kind of energy all along.

What Do You Do After Achieving Your Dream?

Shawn Johnson appeared on and won ABC's *Dancing with the Stars* in 2009. Her entrepreneurial drive continued to be unstoppable, just as her athletic drive was. Johnson has written books, is a motivational speaker, and has a large social media following along with a YouTube channel. Shawn and her husband (Andrew East, a professional football player) live in Nashville and are the proud parents of two children. Life is golden indeed.

Smashing Trains as a Spectator Sport

Who knew railroad history would include the staging of head-on train collisions for thrill-seeking audiences at state fairs and other events nationwide? It took an Iowan like Joseph S. Connolly to come up with such a wild idea to attract more people to the Iowa State Fair in 1932.

His idea for this grandstand spectacle was to stage a planned collision of two steam-powered locomotives. This crash took on an election theme, as a Herbert Hoover train was pitted against a Franklin Delano Roosevelt train. (Spoiler alert: Roosevelt won by a landslide in the real election that year; there are no records of which train "won.")

Here's what Connolly planned: two locomotives facing each other on opposite ends of the track, each traveling at 50 mph with the four engineers jumping out just before the two trains hit each other head-on—and of course, a grandstand filled with people watching. Forty-five thousand spectators had to be held back from getting too close to the crash site as fire spread from one engine to the other.

The over-the-top spectacles Connolly had been producing since 1896 earned him the nickname "Head-On Joe" for his famous train-crashing performances. If you're wondering why he did this, it was simple: "Somewhere in the makeup of every normal person there lurks the suppressed desire to smash things up." There's a huge contingency of monster truck jam fans today who would agree with him.

Head-On Joe was so skilled at staging collisions that he even holds a Guinness World Record for "most trains wrecked." Between 1896 and 1932 he staged 73 deliberate head-on collisions between trains for large crowds of spectators. He repeated his tried-and-true format all over the

Joe Connolly staged huge train wrecks for spectators to watch and used trains such as this steam locomotive from 1930. Courtesy of Wikimedia Commons

US, even "spicing things up a bit" by writing opposing names of political or social positions on the two trains. Supporters then cheered for their chosen train.

The staged train wreck at the Iowa State Fair in 1932 was Connolly's last performance. As the trains met, debris flew and metal screeched . . . and Head-On Joe was reported to have calmly walked away, saying, "Well, that's that."

It was the height of the Great Depression, and staged train wrecks had lost their popularity. Wrecking old but otherwise useful locomotives was viewed as wasteful, and the fair just wasn't bringing in the crowds that it once had. Destroying trains for fun had become an old trend. But Head-On Joe sure had a good ride at the height of its popularity.

Inventing the Butterfly

David A. Armbruster, the first swim coach and head of the University of Iowa swim team in the 1930s, was pondering a way to make the breaststroke faster and more efficient. He modified the arm movements so swimmers would pull their arms above the water instead of below it. He was working with Jack Sieg, one of his students on the swim team, and Sieg invented an underwater kicking style, undulating his body and kicking with both legs at the same time. Put together, they perfected a technique for a new way to move a body through water. Armbruster liked the name he gave it: the "dolphin fishtail butterfly swimming stroke."

Fortunately, the abbreviated name of "butterfly" stuck, and for the next few decades, Armbruster tried to get the swimming world to accept this new stroke. However, coaches around the world who had excellent breaststroke swimmers on their teams were very much against changing swimming rules to allow competition in the new event.

Armbruster persevered, though, and in 1952, the butterfly was finally recognized as its own style with its own set of rules. In 1956 (with the help of European swimmers and coaches), the butterfly stroke was finally added to the list of Olympic events.

David A. Armbruster, University of Iowa swim coach who developed the butterfly stroke, University of Iowa, 1940s. Courtesy of The University of Iowa Libraries, Frederick W. Kent photograph collection

Dolphin Kicks and Butterfly Arms

What's the most difficult swimming stroke to learn? Experts say it's the butterfly and compare it to the age-old grade school challenge: patting your head and rubbing your stomach simultaneously. The dolphin kick that involves a "wave" that goes through the swimmer's body will determine how fast a swimmer cuts through the water. The smoother it is, the faster the swimmer. Paired with the butterfly arm motion of pulling through the water, this stroke demands coordination. When done correctly, it's poetry in motion.

Swimmer demonstrates the arm movements of the butterfly stroke. Courtesy of Wikimedia Commons

According to the International Swimming Hall of Fame, Armbruster was "a coach's coach as well as a swimmer's coach." His ideas on technique, his turning out great swim teams at Iowa for 30 years, and his involvement as president of the College Coaches Association in 1938 are some of the reasons he appealed to coaches and swimmers alike. He developed national champions and several Olympic swimmers at Iowa and is best known for writing *Swimming & Diving*, the accepted textbook on competitive swimming.

Coach Armbruster passed away in 1985 at the age of 94. If you don't remember him for anything else, just think of his name—he developed the "arm" part of the butterfly stroke.

Jump Around

As a young boy, George Nissen watched in awe as the trapeze artists ended their act with a high dive into a huge net that caught them and, much like a spring, sent them flying back into the air. By the time Nissen was in high school, he had fashioned his own "practice" net. The rebound was what interested him most, because if a person could rebound high enough, there was an opportunity to perform acrobatic stunts in midair.

George Nissen on his trampoline.
Courtesy of Dian Nissen

After high school Nissen attended the University of Iowa, where he excelled in gymnastics and tumbling. He won the National Tumbling Championship in his sophomore, junior, and senior years. During his senior year, he joined the Iowa swim team because they needed a diver. At the end of that year, he was not only the national tumbling champion, but also an All-American in diving!

Practice makes perfect, and Nissen never missed an opportunity to perfect his skills. He said, "Each night at the University of Iowa, when we finished our workouts—even in the dead of winter with snow covering the ground—I would go to the football field and do a row of back handsprings the length of the field."

After college, Nissen went to Mexico and put on acrobatic and diving exhibitions, and he also dove for the Mexican government in what was the forerunner of the Pan-American Games. He returned to the US and continued his performing career, putting on over 2,000 exhibitions across the country until World War II broke out.

By this time, he had tinkered with and finally perfected his rebounding apparatus, naming it the "trampoline," from the Spanish word *trampolina*, which means diving board. He registered "trampoline" as his trademark for 15 years before allowing it into the public domain.

A preflight instructor in the Navy, Nissen went on after the war to form the Nissen Trampoline Company, installed trampolines in 10,000 schools and camps, and took the sport worldwide. He developed and owned a gymnastic equipment company in Japan, expanding markets and the product line to include a wide variety of gymnastic and athletic equipment such as parallel bars, horses, balance beams, tumbling/wrestling mats, electronic scoreboards, basketball backboards, and table-tennis tables. At the end of the 1960s, the Nissen company was the largest manufacturer of gymnastic equipment in the world.

Two Natural Jumpers

As part of George Nissen's advertising for his new invention, he rented a kangaroo named Victoria in 1960 so he could train her for a week. He wanted to be able to hop with her on a trampoline he set up in Central Park. Nissen clasped her front paws so she wouldn't box him and together, they learned to bounce in time.

This photograph was just what he was looking for. Not only that, but it achieved the publicity he wanted to establish the trampoline as a global phenomenon.

Courtesy of Dian Nissen

For the Love of Baseball

Sometimes ordinary people with an ordinary passion can do extraordinary things. This was the case with Harris "Shooky" Fink of New Albin. An elementary school janitor, Shooky lived and breathed baseball. He volunteered time as a baseball coach and peppered his everyday conversations with talk of the sport.

His love for the game started when he was a young boy. He and his brother would hoe into the family garden until they were hidden by the cornfield and then take off to play baseball somewhere. In the winter, they'd play ball in the basement. Shooky played in the minor leagues for a short time and might have gone further if it weren't for his bad heart. He discovered he had a heart valve problem that made his heart "gurgle when he ran."

What he could do, however, was inspire others. He loved baseball and he loved kids. When he was living in Chicago in the 1940s and working as a machinist, he taught some of the neighborhood kids the fine art of playing baseball on a lot near his apartment building. When a neighbor who worked nights complained about the noise to the Chicago police, they came to investigate. They saw the makeshift ballfield and figured the constant ballgames helped to keep vandalism down. Shooky received a commendation instead of a citation.

When he moved back home to New Albin, he brought his love of the game with him. He also built a baseball field right on top of the spot where his family's huge garden used to be. And the kids just showed up—all ages at all times—and Shooky was out there coaching them. From 3-year-olds whose gloves were bigger than their heads to high school standouts wanting to glean more baseball wisdom, the kids were there for a daily 11 a.m. practice.

Shooky was there every day—even almost missing his only daughter's wedding because practice ran late. He instilled in kids the confidence they needed to do the best they could, and then some. Through games and scrimmages, he found what worked best for kids and went with it.

Shooky Finch coached Little League teams for decades and turned kids into future members of championship baseball teams in high school. And he left a legacy that has instilled in generations not only a love of the game, but a love of life.

Known as "Mr. Baseball" in New Albin for over 30 years, Harris "Shooky" Fink simply loved baseball and taught others to love it, too. Courtesy of Dana Fink

Coaching Legends Begins with Being One

Dan Gable: wrestler, Olympic gold medalist, and coach. Courtesy of Wikimedia Commons

Gannett News Service named him the top wrestler of the 20th century. He was also honored as one of the top 100 US Olympians of all time. He's the namesake of the National Wrestling Hall of Fame Dan Gable Museum in Waterloo. Dan Gable is simply a wrestling legend.

As many accolades as he accumulated over the years, it's difficult to pinpoint whether he was a better wrestler or a better coach. In the world of wrestling, he is certainly a rarity.

Born in 1948 to a father who was an investor and real estate salesman and a mother who was a homemaker, Gable had an older sister who was tragically murdered in the family's house while he and his parents were away on a fishing trip. Gable said his life tightened up after his sister was gone, and he focused on wrestling as a consolation.

His high school record was amazing; he went 64-0 with 25 pins, and his Iowa State record also surpassed his expectations. He won title after title, including Most Outstanding Wrestler of the NCAA Tournament in his junior year. However, in his senior year, he experienced something he wasn't used to: defeat. He bounced back a couple of weeks later, winning nationals. Looking back, he admitted he needed that defeat to help him get to the Olympics and dominate once he was there. Gable won the gold medal in the 1972 Munich Olympics, pinning three of six opponents.

Following the Olympics, Gable returned to Iowa to be the assistant wrestling coach for the University of Iowa and the head coach not long afterward. He coached his Hawkeye wrestlers to win like he once did, guiding them to national championships time after time.

And then his body needed attention. Between a hip replacement surgery and dozens of knee and back surgeries, he was no longer able to get down on the mat to demonstrate moves to his team. His next move was retirement.

Gable vowed at his retirement press conference that he wouldn't get too far away from wrestling and went on to be head coach for the 1999 World Cup and co-coach of the 2000 US Olympic Freestyle Team. Today, he is a motivational speaker, sharing his life experiences and helping people find success in their everyday lives.

From the "greatest amateur wrestler this country has ever produced" to Olympic gold medalist to coach of Olympians, Dan Gable set the bar high for himself and future wrestlers.

The Dan Gable Museum, operated by the National Wrestling Hall of Fame in Waterloo. Courtesy of Wikimedia Commons

This is what RAGBRAI is all about—riding bikes across the great state of Iowa. Courtesy of RAGBRAI

The Greatest Bike Ride Ever

When two friends came up with the idea to have a casual bike ride across Iowa over the course of six days, they didn't know it would be a tradition for over 50 years and turn into the oldest, largest, and longest bicycle touring event in the world.

John Karras and Don Kaul were columnists for the *Des Moines Register* in 1973 when Karras suggested to Kaul that he ride his bike across Iowa and write columns about what he saw. Kaul agreed, but only if Karras would go with him. They planned a route from Sioux City to Davenport August 26–31 with stops along the way including Storm Lake, Fort Dodge, Ames, Des Moines, and Williamsburg. They invited the public to join them, and around 300 people showed up for the ride, with 114 riders making it the entire distance that year.

The name of that first ride was "The Great Six-Day Bicycle Ride," and for the third year's event the name changed to "RAGBRAI," which stands for "*Register*'s Annual Great Bike Ride Across Iowa." Since that original bike ride, thousands of people from all over the world have joined in this iconic event. Towns along the way pull out all the stops, and what was once just a little bike ride to gain some additional material for *Register* columns became so much more.

Courtney Crowder, co-director of *Shift: The RAGBRAI Documentary*, said that RAGBRAI represents different things for the riders. In a news segment for a Des Moines TV station, Crowder said, "It's about unlocking and embracing whatever you put on hold in your life to come to Iowa at the end of July and ride across this state."

The route changes every year, but certain traditions remain. It always begins on the west side of the state and moves to the east. To signify the start of the ride, bikers first dip their back tires in the Missouri River (or one of its tributaries) and then dip their front tires in the Mississippi River to signify the end of the ride.

For a real adventure and a story to tell your grandchildren someday, this is the bike ride to take. Although other states have followed suit, RAGBRAI is the biggest, and Iowans would tell you it's also the very best.

RAGBRAI at a Glance

- **Since its beginning, RAGBRAI has been to all 99 counties in Iowa.**
- **There is now a limit of 8,500 riders to maintain a sense of control and limit the number of injuries.**
- **Nationwide broadcasts, magazines, newspapers, and social media channels have covered this annual event.**
- **Over 330,000 cyclists have hit the road since RAGBRAI's initial bike ride.**
- **The ride was canceled for the first (and so far only) time in 2020 due to the COVID-19 pandemic.**

Endnotes

Chapter 1
Iowa Firsts

First Robbery of a Moving Train

Foxx, S. (2022, March 1). Did you know Jesse James and his gang robbed a train in Iowa? KCRR 97.7. kcrr.com/did-you-know-jesse-james-and-his-gang-robbed-a-train-in-iowa/

Pfingsten, B. (Ed.). (2024, March 6). First train robbery in the West historical marker. Historical Marker. hmdb.org/m.asp?m=34280

Compute This!

Rolls, A. (n.d.). The Atanasoff Berry Computer: The controversy behind the world's first digital computer. Jameco Electronics. jameco.com/Jameco/workshop/rollcall/first-digital-computer.html

Schmidt, D. A. (1996). Iowa pride. Iowa State University Press.

First Airline Stewardess in the US

Bonney, Margaret Atherton. (Ed). Ellen Church: The flying nurse, The Goldfinch 2, no. 1 (September 1980): 14 –15.

Ellen Church and the advent of the sky girls. US Federal Aviation Administration. (n.d.). faa.gov/sites/faa.gov/files/about/history/pioneers/Ellen_Church_and_the_Advent_of_the_Sky_Girls.pdf

Ellen Church: The flying nurse. Iowa PBS. (n.d.). iowapbs.org/iowapathways/mypath/2493/ellen-church-flying-nurse

Latson, J. (2015, May 15). Flight attendants of history: How the first stewardess got her job. Time. time.com/3847732/first-stewardess-ellen-church

I Taught Amelia Earhart to Fly!

Snook, Neta. Ameshistory.org. (n.d.). ameshistory.org/content/neta-snook

Champion of Women's Right to Vote

About Carrie. Carrie Chapman Catt Girlhood Home. (n.d.). catt.org/carrie/about

Schmidt, D. A. (1996). Iowa pride. Iowa State University Press.

Van Voris, J. (1996). Carrie Chapman Catt: A public life. Feminist Press at the City University of New York.

Get into Align(ment)

Schmidt, D. A. (1996). Iowa pride. Iowa State University Press.

The Palmer family. Palmer College of Chiropractic. (2024, July 8). palmer.edu/about-palmer/palmer-college-history/the-palmer-family

Best Thing Since Sliced Bread

Baking Hall of Fame 2008: Otto Rohwedder. American Society of Baking. (n.d.). asbe.org/bhof-2008-orohwedder

Kelly, K. (2023, February 18). Bread-slicing machine: The inventor. America Comes Alive. americacomesalive.com/bread-slicing-machine-inventor

Nix, E. (2015, January 16). Who invented sliced bread? History.com. history.com/news/who-invented-sliced-bread

Home of the American Cream Draft Horse

Anon. (2023, June 9). Rare draft horses being celebrated in Jewell, Ellsworth, Radcliffe. radioiowa.com/2023/06/09/rare-draft-horses-being-celebrated-in-jewell-ellsworth-radcliffe

History. American Cream Draft Horse Association. (n.d.). acdha.org/history

It's a Bird! It's a Plane! It's a . . . Meteorite!

Estherville meteorite. Estherville Area Chamber of Commerce. (n.d.). estherville.org/estherville-meteorite.html#:~:text=On%20May%2010%2C%201879%2C%20a,15%20feet%20in%20the%20ground.

Swanger, M. (2017, April 29). Fireball from outer space. Iowa History Journal. iowahistoryjournal.com/fireball-outer-space

Tractor Power

Froelich Tractor Museum. Froelich Tractor Museum. (n.d.). froelichtractor.com

Schmidt, D. A. (1996). Iowa pride. Iowa State University Press.

Ease the Pain

Buffered aspirin is discovered. University of Iowa Carver College of Medicine. (n.d.). medicine.uiowa.edu/content/buffered-aspirin-discovered

Schmidt, D. A. (1996). Iowa pride. Iowa State University Press.

Ice Cream Capital of the World

About. Blue Bunny. (n.d.). bluebunny.com/about

Birthplace of the Greatest Show on Earth

Munson, K. (2017, January 18). Iowa is the true birthplace of the dying Ringling Bros. circus. Des Moines Register. desmoinesregister.com/story/news/local/columnists/kyle-munson/2017/01/17/ringling-bros-circus-dying-iowa-true-birthplace/96675950

Rushing, T. (2024, February 13). Iowa weird: Cascade, the small Iowa town that saved the circus. Iowa Starting Line. iowastartingline.com/2022/06/01/iowa-weird-cascade-ringling-brothers-circus-history

The Ringling Bros and Cascade History. City of Cascade. (n.d.). tricountyhistoricalsociety.com/ringling-bros

First Fast Food Franchise . . . Made Right!

Hall, C. M. (2023, September 8). Fred L. Angell doing business as Maid Rite. IAGen Web

Project/Muscatine County Iowa. iagenweb.org/muscatine/articles/angell-maidrite_story.htm
How We Maid History. Maid-Rite. (n.d.). maid-rite.com
Schmidt, D. A. (1996). Iowa pride. Iowa State University Press.
Walker, S. (2021, September 7). Muscatine born and bred Maid-Rite named iconic postgame spot in Iowa. Voice Of Muscatine. voiceofmuscatine.com/2021/09/07/muscatine-born-and-bred-maid-rite-ranked-as-iconic-postgame-spot-in-iowa/

He Made 'Em Scream for "I-Scream!"

A great Danish American birthday—Christian Kent Nelson. National Foundation for Danish America. (n.d.). tockify.com/danishamerica/detail/556/1836367200000
Guide to the Eskimo Pie corporation records, 1921–1996. Eskimo Pie Corporation Records Collection: NMAH.AC.0553. (n.d.). sova.si.edu/record/nmah.ac.0553
Los Angeles Times. (1992, March 10). Eskimo pie inventor C. Nelson dies at 98: Obituary: His chocolate-covered ice cream bar, developed in 1921, became a confectionary institution. latimes.com/archives/la-xpm-1992-03-10-me-3613-story.html

A (Delicious) Apple a Day

Hawkeye Apple. Trapple Orchard. (n.d.). trappleorchard.com/hawkeye-apple.html
Schmidt, D. A. (1996). Iowa pride. Iowa State University Press.

The Mother of 4-H

Field, Jessie. The Corn Lady: The Story of a Country Teacher's Work. United States: A. Flanagan Company, 1911.
Schmidt, D. A. (1996). Iowa pride. Iowa State University Press.
Shambaugh, Jessie Field, 1881–1971. ArchivesSpace at the University of Iowa. (n.d.). aspace.lib.uiowa.edu/agents/people/1592

Keep Poppin'

Our Story. JOLLY TIME®. (2024, May 31). jollytime.com

From First to Last One-of-a-Kind Hotel

History of the Historic Park Inn Hotel. Wright on the Park. (n.d.). wrightonthepark.org/wright-on-the-park-history
Piper, A. (n.d.). A peek at the Historic Park Inn in Mason City, Iowa. Follow the Piper. followthepiper.com/the-historic-park-inn-a-look-inside

Chapter 2
Famous Iowans

America's Painter Laureate

Biel, S. (2006). American Gothic: A life of America's most famous painting. W.W. Norton.
Hoving, T., & Wood, G. (2005). American Gothic: The biography of Grant Wood's American masterpiece. Chamberlain Bros.
Schmidt, D. A. (1996). Iowa pride. Iowa State University Press.
Whye, M. (2020). Detour Iowa: Historic destinations. The History Press.

Spaced Out

Berz, N. (2024, April 17). Peggy Whitson breaks the glass ceiling, lands among the stars. The Rice Thresher. ricethresher.org/article/2024/04/peggy-whitson-breaks-the-glass-ceiling-lands-among-the-stars
Cichon, B. (2024, March 26). Curious Iowa: What are Iowa's connections to space science and exploration? The Gazette. thegazette.com/curious-iowa/curious-iowa-what-are-iowas-connections-to-space-science-and-exploration
National 4-H Council. (2022, November 28). How do you become an astronaut? Astronaut Peggy Whitson on her journey to space. 4-h.org/about/blog/how-do-you-become-an-astronaut-astronaut-peggy-whitson-on-her-journey-to-space x

The World's Worst Sister Act

El-Hai, J. (2019, September 6). The Cherry Sisters: Good or bad? el-hai.com/blog/2012/6/6/the-cherry-sisters-good-or-bad.html
Jarrell, M. W. (n.d.). Aug 12, 1933, page 12, Santa Cruz Evening News. Newspapers.com. newspapers.com/image/50534694/?clipping_id=38895403&fcfToken=eyJhbGciOiJIUzI1NiIsInR5cCI6IkpXVCJ9.eyJmcmVlLXZpZXctaWQiOjUwNTM0Njk0LCJpYXQiOjE3MjMzNDAzNjAsImV4cCI6MTcyMzQyNjc2MH0.TokI06ovZWeQpL6lunPQ7U3QRk0S_FU9dgThOmvHjQk
Pohlen, J. (2005). Oddball Iowa: A guide to some really strange places. Chicago Review Press.
Weeks, L. (2015, June 27). The Cherry Sisters: Worst act ever? National Public Radio. npr.org/sections/npr-history-dept/2015/06/27/417439984/the-cherry-sisters-worst-act-ever

Hard-Working Actor from the Heartland

Brainard, R. (2022, August 30). Ashton Kutcher shares stories about growing up in Iowa. 98.1 KHAK. khak.com/ashton-kutcher-shares-stories-about-growing-up-in-iowa-watch/
Tatham, P. (2023, December 11). Ashton Kutcher: Biography. HELLO! hellomagazine.com/profiles/201110201008/ashton-kutcher/
Thole, E. (2022, November 4). Cedar Rapids on screen. Cedar Rapids Tourism Office. tourismcedarrapids.com/blog/cedar-rapids-on-screen

What a Voice!
Schmidt, D. A. (1996). Iowa pride. Iowa State University Press.
Simon Estes: From Centerville to center stage. (2023, September 25). Our Iowa Heritage. ouriowaheritage.com/our-iowa-heritage-simon-estes
Simon Estes's biography. The HistoryMakers. (n.d.). thehistorymakers.org/biography/simon-estes-41

Big Band Man
Biography.com Editors. (2014, April 2). Glenn Miller Biography. Biography.com. biography.com/musicians/glenn-miller
Ruane, M. E. (2019, December 24). 75 years ago, Iowa native and big band leader Glenn Miller vanished on a flight over the English Channel. The Gazette. thegazette.com/people-places/75-years-ago-iowa-native-and-big-band-leader-glenn-miller-vanished-on-a-flight-over-the-english-cha
Schmidt, D. A. (1996). Iowa pride. Iowa State University Press.

Snap, Crackle, Pop Treats
A famous treat. Iowa State University College of Human Sciences. (n.d.). hs.iastate.edu/recipes/a-famous-treat
For the Al: Mildred day. Jay P. Greene's Blog. (2019, October 31). jaypgreene.com/2019/10/31/for-the-al-mildred-day
From the archives: Love Rice Krispies Treats? You have an Iowan to thank. Des Moines Register. (2021, June 15). desmoinesregister.com/story/entertainment/dining/2017/09/21/archives-love-rice-krispies-treats-you-have-iowan-thank/686025001

Keokuk's Writing Son
1869: Mark Twain comes to Iowa City. Our Iowa Heritage. (2024, April 28). ouriowaheritage.com/mark-twain-2
From the archives: Mark Twain made his debut as a speaker, and sold his first written work, in Iowa. Des Moines Register. (2021, October 21). desmoinesregister.com/story/life/2021/10/21/famous-iowans-mark-twain-sold-his-first-written-work-iowa-samuel-clemens-keokuk-muscatine/8490389002
Mark Twain historical marker. Historical Marker. (2022, December 18). hmdb.org/m.asp?m=178943

Just Like Nancy Drew
Fisher, J. (n.d.). Just the facts about Millie: The Mildred A. Wirt Benson Website. nancydrewsleuth.com/milliemedia.html
From the Archives: Mystery solved: an Iowan was behind iconic "Nancy Drew" series. The Des Moines Register. (2021, February 13). desmoinesregister.com/story/news/2017/12/11/archives-nancy-drew-author-mildred-wirt-benson-ladora-iowa/941906001

The Lawnmower Man
Stilwell, B. (2023, September 8). That time a 73-year-old World War II vet drove 240 miles on a riding mower. Military.com. military.com/off-duty/movies/2023/09/08/time-73-year-old-world-war-ii-vet-drove-240-miles-riding-mower.html
The straight story: Across Iowa on a Lawnmower. The Attic. (2024, January 11). theattic.space/home-page-blogs/2023/9/29/8jx36sr3vtvluzdk1uj4uhcu10jvdy

Buffalo Bill's Wild West
Buffalo Bill Cody history. Scott County, Iowa. (2016, June 14). scottcountyiowa.gov/conservation/buffalo-bill-cody-homestead/buffalo-bill-history
From the archives: Wild west icon and showman "Buffalo" Bill Cody. Des Moines Register. (2018, September 11). desmoinesregister.com/story/news/2018/02/26/famous-iowan-buffalo-bill-cody-leclaire-iowa/375034002
History of Buffalo Bill. Buffalo Bill Museum & Grave. (2023, January 19). buffalobill.org/history-research/history-of-buffalo-bill
Schmidt, D. A. (1996). Iowa pride. Iowa State University Press.

He's a Music Man
Cabaniss, M. (2023). Miracle of the music man: The classic American story of Meredith Willson. Blackstone Publishing.
Pohlen, J. (2005). Oddball Iowa: A guide to some really strange places. Chicago Review Press.
Robert "Meredith" Willson. IAGen Web Project/Cerro Gordo County. (n.d.). iagenweb.org/cerrogordo/bios/bio-wilsonmeredith.htm
Schmidt, D. A. (1996). Iowa pride. Iowa State University Press.
Willson, M. (2009). And there I stood with my piccolo. University of Minnesota Press.

More than OK
6 things you should know about Wyatt Earp. History.com. (n.d.) history.com/news/6-things-you-should-know-about-wyatt-earp
Bommersbach, J. (n.d.). Searching for Wyatt Earp as a boy. True West Magazine. truewestmagazine.com/article/searching-for-wyatt-earp-as-a-boy
Boyhood home of Wyatt Earp re-opens in Pella. Oskaloosa Herald. (2021, May 14). oskaloosa.com/iowa/boyhood-home-of-wyatt-earp-re-opens-in-pella/article_8ae3c3bc-b4c4-11eb-add9-f37e6eea05ab.html
Whye, M. (2020). Detour Iowa: Historic destinations. History Press.
Wyatt Berry Stapp Earp. Teaching Iowa History. (n.d.). teachingiowahistory.org/iowa-stories/wyatt-berry-stapp-earp

Advice Queens

Baron, M. (2022, April 15). The rivalry of Dear Abby and Ann Landers. Book Riot. bookriot.com/dear-abby-and-ann-landers/

From the Archives: Competition between Iowa sisters who penned Dear Abby, Ann Landers fueled advice columns. The Des Moines Register. (2021, September 24). desmoinesregister.com/story/entertainment/2021/09/20/famous-iowans-sioux-city-twin-sisters-penned-dear-abby-ann-landers-advice-columns/8418136002/

Pohlen, J. (2005). Oddball Iowa: A guide to some really strange places. Chicago Review Press.

Schmidt, D. A. (1996). Iowa pride. Iowa State University Press.

We Stick Together

Sullivan Brothers Iowa Veterans Museum. Grout Museum District. (n.d.). groutmuseumdistrict.org/sites-exhibits/sullivan-brothers-iowa-veterans-museum/default.aspx

The Sullivan brothers and the assignment of family members. US Navy Naval History and Heritage Command (n.d.). history.navy.mil/browse-by-topic/disasters-and-phenomena/the-sullivan-brothers-and-the-assignment-of-family-members0.html

The Great Humanitarian

Schmidt, D. A. (1996). Iowa pride. Iowa State University Press.

Speeches. Hoover Presidential Foundation. (2024, August 2). hooverpresidentialfoundation.org/speeches

The American Duke

Erickson, L. (2017). Iowa: Off the beaten path: Discover your fun. Globe Pequot.

John Wayne Birthplace & Museum. (2024, June 26). johnwaynebirthplace.museum

Schmidt, D. A. (1996). Iowa pride. Iowa State University Press.

Whye, M. (2020). Detour Iowa: Historic destinations. The History Press.

Winterset, Iowa: The birthplace of John Wayne. Wander Wisdom. (n.d.). wanderwisdom.com/travel-destinations/Winterset--Iowa---The-birthplace-of-that-great-patriot--John-Wayne

Mr. State Fair

Bill Riley Talent show. The Cedar County Fair. (2024, June 7). thecedarcountyfair.com/bill-riley-talent-show

Munson, K. (2016, August 13). Last words of "Mr. State Fair" arrive a decade after his death. Des Moines Register. desmoinesregister.com/story/news/local/columnists/kyle-munson/2016/08/13/last-words-mr-state-fair-arrive-decade-after-his-death/88631008

Porter, S. A. (2020, August 19). Iowa PBS host Bill Riley is "celebrating the fair" with new series showcasing event's best moments. Des Moines Register. desmoinesregister.com/story/entertainment/arts/arts-in-iowa/2020/08/19/iowa-pbs-bill-riley-share-half-century-state-fair-highlights/3377708001

Heroine on the Rails

About Kate Shelley. Kate Shelley. (n.d.). kateshelley.com/about-kate.html

Bannister, M. (2023). Secret Iowa: A Guide to the Weird, Wonderful, and Obscure. Reedy Press.

Jones, E., Dr. Science, & Thorkelson, B. (2010). Iowa curiosities: Quirky characters, roadside oddities & other offbeat stuff. Globe Pequot Press.

Kate Shelley Bridge. Iowa PBS. (n.d.). iowapbs.org/education/findiowa/media/9568/kate-shelley-bridge

Mason, K. (2023, July 6). Iowa history daily: July 6—Kate Shelley crosses the High Bridge. Notes on Iowa. notesoniowa.com/post/iowa-history-daily-july-6-kate-shelley-crosses-the-high-bridge

Chapter 3
Iowa Curiosities and Oddities

Iowa's "Black Utopia"

Bannister, M. (2023). Secret Iowa: A guide to the weird, wonderful, and obscure. Reedy Press.

Buxton: A lost utopia. State Historical Society of Iowa. (n.d.). history.iowa.gov/history/education/educator-resources/primary-source-sets/buxton-lost-utopia

Digging for history: A look back at Iowa's majority-black mining town. weareiowa.com. (n.d.). weareiowa.com/article/news/community/digging-for-history-a-look-at-iowas-black-majority-coal-mining-town-black-history-month-mining-buxton/524-96aa7fee-c0c9-4f87-b59a-f1603b23f1f8

POWs and a Nativity

Bannister, M. (2023). Secret Iowa: A Guide to the Weird, Wonderful, and Obscure. Reedy Press.

Hughes, M. (2022, December 14). Lansing-based producers tell story of German POWs in Midwest. Lansing State Journal. lansingstatejournal.com/story/entertainment/movies/2022/12/14/silent-in-algona-tells-story-of-world-war-ii-pows-in-small-iowa-town/69719481007

Jones, E., Dr. Science, & Thorkelson, B. (2010). Iowa curiosities: Quirky characters, roadside oddities & other offbeat stuff. Globe Pequot Press.

Lewis, R. (n.d.). Algona Nativity Scene. Omeka RSS. algonanativityscene.omeka.net

NATIVITY. Camp Algona POW Museum. (n.d.). pwcampalgona.org/nativity

Pohlen, J. (2005). Oddball Iowa: A guide to some really strange places. Chicago Review Press.

Hiccups That Set a World Record

Ferris, Mike (2020, June 11). The Iowa man who had hiccupps for 68 years. 94.1 KRNA. krna.com/the-iowa-man-who-had-hiccupps-for-68-years

Gormly, Kellie B. (2022, June 13). The curious case of Charles Osborne, who hiccupped for 68 years straight. Smithsonian. smithsonianmag.com/history/the-curious-case-of-charles-osborne-who-hiccuped-for-68-years-straight-180980232

Longest attack of hiccups. Guinness World Records (1999, February 2). guinnessworldrecords.com/world-records/67619-longest-attack-of-hiccups

The Geyser That Wouldn't Quit

Gott, Andy. (2022, August 27). Did you know Iowa has a giant dormant geyser? KXRB 1140 AM/100.1 FM. kxrb.com/did-you-know-iowa-has-a-giant-dormant-geyser

Jones, E., Dr Science, & Thorkelson, B. (2010). Iowa curiosities: Quirky characters, roadside oddities & other offbeat stuff. Globe Pequot Press.

Our Town Belle Plaine: Jumbo Geyser. KCRG-TV9 (n.d.). youtube.com/watch?v=rfv9kqVRe5o

Time Machine: Old jumbo. (2015, February 7). The Gazette. thegazette.com/news/time-machine-old-jumbo

The Crookedest Street in the World

History, heritage & Snake Alley. City of Burlington, Iowa. (n.d.). burlingtoniowa.org/2311/History-Heritage-Snake-Alley

Snake alley: A very crooked street, Burlington, Iowa. RoadsideAmerica.com. (n.d.). roadsideamerica.com/story/11322#google_vignette

Snake alley: Burlington, Iowa: Travel Iowa. (n.d.). traveliowa.com/places/snake-alley/690

Snake alley. Greater Burlington Partnership. (n.d.). greaterburlington.com/convention-and-visitors-bureau/explore/snake-alley

Delicious Mobster Hideout

Brennan, P. (2024, August 14). Fire destroys the Lighthouse Inn, a Cedar Rapids landmark and one of Iowa's oldest restaurants. Little Village. littlevillagemag.com/fire-destroys-lighthouse-inn/

Lighthouse Inn Supper Club home page (n.d.). crlighthouseinn12.homesteadcloud.com

Maas, E. (2024, August 15). Community reacts to loss of Lighthouse Inn. KWWL. kwwl.com/news/cedar-rapids/community-reacts-to-loss-of-lighthouse-inn/article_14be7228-5a83-11ef-a6e5-5bf9d6d6280e.html

Magaraci, K. (n.d.). Iowa's very first supper club has literally been around forever. Only In Your State. onlyinyourstate.com/iowa/lighthouse-inn-supper-club-ia/

Pratt, R. (2024, August 14). Historic Lighthouse Inn destroyed in fire. Corridor Business Journal. corridorbusiness.com/lighthouse-inn-fire-destroyed

The Day the Music Died

Hohn, L. (2024, April 19). Clear Lake breaks ground on Surf Ballroom Music Enrichment Center and surf district revitalization. Clear Lake Iowa. clearlakeiowa.com/clear-lake-breaks-ground-on-surf-ballroom-music-enrichment-center-and-surf-district-revitalization/

Pohlen, J. (2005). Oddball Iowa: A guide to some really strange places. Chicago Review Press.

Surf ballroom breaks ground on music enrichment and immersive center. KIMT3 (n.d.). kimt.com/news/surf-ballroom-breaks-ground-on-music-enrichment-and-immersive-center/article_fd13b794-fe4a-11ee-ad1f-33f58f72210e.html

Surf Ballroom. US Department of the Interior: National Park Service. nps.gov/places/surf-ballroom.htm

Timeline. Surf Ballroom. (n.d.). surfballroom.com/timeline.html

Whye, M. (2020). Detour Iowa: Historic destinations. History Press.

Build It and They Will Come

Field of dreams getting $80 million makeover, including 9 new youth ballfields. CBS News (n.d.). cbsnews.com/chicago/news/field-of-dreams-expansion-dyersville-iowa

Field of dreams, Dyersville, Iowa. RoadsideAmerica.com. (n.d.-a). roadsideamerica.com/story/2079

Visit Us. *Field of Dreams* Movie Site. (n.d.). fieldofdreamsmoviesite.com/visit

Yoder, B. & Hensley, A. (2023, January 19). Is there a Field of Dreams game in Iowa this year? Here are 17 things you should know. Des Moines Register. desmoinesregister.com/story/sports/2021/08/11/things-know-field-of-dreams-movie-dyersville-iowa-mlb-game-yankees-white-sox/5557003001

Missing Monet in a Mailbox

Iowa town feels it lost more than a painting. Chicago Tribune. (2021, August 9). chicagotribune.com/1987/03/23/iowa-town-feels-it-lost-more-than-a-painting

Mason, K. (2024, March 19). Iowa history daily: March 19—Marshalltown's Monet heist. Notes on Iowa. notesoniowa.com/post/iowa-history-daily-march-19-marshalltown-s-monet-heist

Missing Monet turns up in Mailbox. UPI. (1988, March 8). upi.com/Archives/1988/03/08/Missing-Monet-turns-up-in-mailbox/4443573800400

Which Came First—the Song or the Church?

History. The Little Brown Church in the Vale. (n.d.). littlebrownchurch.org/the-church/history

Little Brown Church in the Vale. Hymntime.com (n.d.). http://hymntime.com/tch/htm/l/i/t/t/l/littlebc.htm

Schaap, James C. (2018, August 8). The Little Brown Church in the Vale. Siouxland Public Media. kwit.org/featured-programs/2018-08-08/the-little-brown-church-in-the-vale

Thompson, R. (2016, December 13). The story behind the song: church in the Wildwood. Bluegrass Today. bluegrasstoday.com/the-story-behind-the-song-church-in-the-wildwood/#google_vignette

Welcome Back, Paddlefish!

Eide, E. (2024, August 14). Native paddlefish will be reintroduced to the Iowa Great Lakes. KTIV. ktiv.com. ktiv.com/2024/08/14/native-paddlefish-will-be-reintroduced-iowa-great-lakes

Fishing. Iowa Department of Natural Resources. (n.d.). iowadnr.gov/Fishing/Iowa-Fish-Species/Fish-Details/SpeciesCode/PAH

Harlow, K. (2020, February 10). Lake monsters. NwestIowa.com. nwestiowa.com/okoboji_magazine/features/lake-monsters/article_789f9aac-6da3-11e8-bb6a-6f33db25fbf4.html

Iowa DNR reintroducing paddlefish to the Iowa Great Lakes. Explore Okoboji. (n.d.). exploreokoboji.com/news/news-stories/iowa-dnr-reintroducing-paddle-fish-to-the-iowa-great-lakes

Lannoo, M. J. (1996). Okoboji wetlands a lesson in natural history. University of Iowa Press.

Schooley, J. (2020, July 6). World record paddlefish: Conspiracies, genetics, and advances in snagging technology. The Fisheries Blog. thefisheriesblog.com/2020/07/06/world-record-paddlefish-conspiracies-genetics-and-advances-in-snagging-technology

Coffin-Making Monks

Iowa monks use natural resources to create wooden caskets. Public News Service. (n.d.). publicnewsservice.org/2024-03-18/arts-and-culture/iowa-monks-use-natural-resources-to-create-wooden-caskets/a89326-1

Kelsey, E. (2024, August 5). "A prayerful environment": Trappist caskets provide "old-world craftsmanship." TelegraphHerald.com. telegraphherald.com/news/tri-state/article_d877fd3e-0934-11ee-a911-a74ec3d9ac33.html

The trappist life. Cistercians of the Strict Observance (Trappists). (2023, March 10). trappists.org/trappist-life

Trappist Caskets (n.d.). trappistcaskets.com/caskets

Trappist caskets. New Melleray Abbey. (n.d.). newmelleray.org/work-4/trappist-caskets-2

Iowa's Only Island City

Kenney, C. (2021, May 12). Iowa's only island city is an hour from the Quad Cities [photos]. B100. b100quadcities.com/iowas-island-city

Kevin Across America (n.d.). Landlocked Iowa has an island town that 500 people live on. youtube.com/watch?v=e4rbIlzQbfI

Lefevers, D. (n.d.). This island in Iowa is an absolute must visit. Only In Your State: Discover Magic in Your Own Backyard. onlyinyourstate.com/iowa/sabula-ia/

Crossing State Lines for Candy

About Palmer. Palmer-Candy. (n.d.). palmercandy.com/pages/about-palmer

Green-Warnstadt, M. (2022, June 7). Palmer Candy Company. Sioux City Public Museum. siouxcitymuseum.org/history-website/palmer-candy-company

How the iconic Twin Bing candy is made. Sioux City Journal (n.d.). youtube.com/watch?v=5PVi7CHR3lo

Ianlefk. (2023, December 25). Palmer's olde tyme candy shoppe. Atlas Obscura. atlasobscura.com/places/palmers-olde-tyme-candy-shoppe-iowa

Magaraci, K. (n.d.). World famous Twin Bing Candy is still made right here in the Hawkeye State. Only In Your State: onlyinyourstate.com/iowa/twin-bings-candy-ia

Glow-in-the-Dark Trail

Decious, E. (2021, June 17). Father's legacy beams from Vinton's glowing trail, longest in U.S. The Gazette. thegazette.com/people-places/glow-in-the-dark-trail-in-vinton-is-longest-in-u-s-honors-resident-who-died-in-january

Nathan's Miles Glow Trail: Shive-Hattery. ShiveHattery. (2023, October 25). shive-hattery.com/nathans-miles-glow-trail

Nathan's Miles Glow Trail: Vinton, Iowa: Travel Iowa. (n.d.). traveliowa.com/places/nathan-s-miles-glow-trail/8536

Phelps, B. (2021, May 28). Vinton is home to the longest glow-in-the-dark trail in the country. KCRG. kcrg.com/2021/05/28/vinton-is-home-to-the-longest-glow-in-the-dark-trail-in-the-country/

Whoa! This glow-in-the-dark trail in Iowa is made with more than a ton of glowing stones. WDSU. (2021, July 1). wdsu.com/article/iowa-glow-in-the-dark-trail/36572851

A Miracle in Stone

Grotto of the Redemption: City of West Bend, Iowa. (2024, July 3). westbendiowa.com/attractions/grotto-of-redemption

Shrine of the Grotto of the Redemption. Rock & Gem Magazine (2023, May 19). rockngem.com/shrine-of-the-grotto-of-the-redemption/#:~:text=The%20Shrine%20of%20the%20Grotto,and%20petrifications%20in%20one%20location

Shrine of the Grotto of the Redemption (2024, July 18). westbendgrotto.com/history

World's largest man-made grotto: World record in West Bend, Iowa. World Record Academy. (2023, June 16). worldrecordacademy.org/2023/6/worlds-largest-man-made-grotto-world-record-in-west-bend-iowa-423257

Chapter 4
Dark Tales

Survivor of the Spirit Lake Massacre

Abbie Gardner Sharp Cabin history. State Historical Society of Iowa. (n.d.). history.iowa.gov/sites/default/files/2022-10/history-sites-abbiegardner-sitehistory.pdf

Abigail Gardner Sharp. US Department of the Interior: National Park Service. (n.d.) nps.gov/people/abigail-gardner-sharp.htm

Gardner-Sharp, A. (1997). History of the Spirit Lake massacre and captivity of Miss Abbie Gardner. Dickinson County Historical Society and Museum Inc.

Pohlen, J. (2005). Oddball Iowa: A guide to some really strange places. Chicago Review Press.

Schaap, J. C. (n.d.). "The day of realization: A review essay of Abbie Gardner's *The Spirit Lake massacre and captivity of Abbie Gardner*." Dordt Digital Collections. digitalcollections.dordt.edu/pro_rege/vol49/iss1/6

Spirit Lake massacre. Teaching Iowa History. (n.d.). teachingiowahistory.org/iowa-stories/spirit-lake-massacre

Axe Murder House

13 of Iowa's most haunted spots. Travel Iowa. (n.d.). traveliowa.com/13-of-iowas-most-haunted

Barreda, V. (2022, June 10). What to know on the anniversary of the 1912 Villisca ax murders. Des Moines Register. desmoinesregister.com/story/news/2022/06/09/1912-villisca-ax-murders-what-to-know-iowa-cold-case/7567590001

The 9 most haunted places in Iowa. Haunted Rooms America. (2024, March 22). hauntedrooms.com/iowa/haunted-places

Villisca Ax Murder House and Museum, Villisca, Iowa. Roadside America. (n.d.). roadsideamerica.com/story/12163

Villisca Ax Murder House, one of Iowa's most haunted locations. We Are Iowa (n.d.). weareiowa.com/article/news/crime/true-crime/villisca-ax-murders-unsolved-111-year-anniversary/524-017c592f-9a74-415b-923a-62ae0d6b9ff6

Villisca Ax murder house: Villisca, Iowa. Travel Iowa. (n.d.). traveliowa.com/places/villisca-axe-murder-house/201

Vyn, K. (2018). Haunted Iowa. Heathcliff Press.

Welcome to the historic Villisca Axe Murder House. US Ghost Adventures. (2024, January 26). usghostadventures.com/villisca-axe-murder-house

A Tale of Two (Haunted) Bridges

13 of Iowa's most haunted spots. Travel Iowa. (n.d.). traveliowa.com/13-of-iowas-most-haunted

Local legends around Iowa's "haunted" locations. Iowa PBS. (n.d.). iowapbs.org/article/8600/local-legends-around-iowas-haunted-locations

The 9 most haunted places in Iowa. Haunted Rooms America. (2024, March 22). hauntedrooms.com/iowa/haunted-places

Beware of the Black Angel

Bannister, M. (2023, August 22). The black angel of Oakland Cemetery: Iowa City, Iowa. Olio in Iowa. olioiniowa.com/blog/oakland-cemeterys-black-angel.

Black angel. The City of Iowa City. (n.d.). iowa-city.org/weblink/0/doc/1481292/Electronic.aspx

Hau, J. (2024, August 19). Top 11 haunts along the Lincoln Highway Heritage Byway: Prairie Rivers of Iowa. prrcd.org/hauntsalongthelincolnhighway

How a black angel statue in Iowa went from heartfelt memorial to spooky legend. KCUR. (2018, July 6). kcur.org/talk-show/2016-10-20/how-a-black-angel-statue-in-iowa-went-from-heartfelt-memorial-to-spooky-legend

Iowa City's infamous Black Angel. Our Iowa Heritage. (2024, April 25). ouriowaheritage.com/black-angel

Jones, E., Dr. Science, & Thorkelson, B. (2010). Iowa curiosities: Quirky characters, roadside oddities & other offbeat stuff. Globe Pequot Press.

Vyn, K. (2018). Haunted Iowa. Heathcliff Press.

The Brady Street Banshee

Pohlen, J. (2005). Oddball Iowa: A guide to some really strange places. Chicago Review Press.

SCblogger. (2014, January 16). Silencing the Banshee of Brady Street. Davenport Public Library. blogs.davenportlibrary.com/sc/2008/10/27/silencing-the-banshee-of-brady-street

Thompson, D. (2024, January 11). Haunted Iowa: 7 places to get your scare on. Stranger Travels USA. strangertravelsusa.com/haunted-iowa/

Vaudeville Ghosts in Cresco

Cresco Theatre & Opera House home page. (n.d.). crescotheatreoperahouse.com

Goldfield, R. (n.d.). The haunted theater in Iowa both history buffs and ghost hunters will love. Only In Your State. onlyinyourstate.com/experiences/iowa/haunted-and-historic-place-ia

Grand Opera House home page. (n.d.). thegrandoperahouse.com.

Iowa's Grand Opera House houses violent attic spirit. Haunted US. (2023, May 1). hauntedus.com/iowa/the-grand-opera-house

The 9 most haunted places in Iowa. Haunted Rooms America. (2024, March 22). hauntedrooms.com/iowa/haunted-places

Lake of the Dead Man

Dead Man's Lake. Iowa Conservation Commission. (n.d.). publications.iowa.gov/40585/1/Dead_Mans_Lake_1983_OCR_.pdf

Pilot Knob State Park. Iowa State Conservation Board. (n.d.). publications.iowa.gov/13251/2/Pilot_Knob_State_Park.pdf

Places to go. Iowa Department of Natural Resources. (n.d.). iowadnr.gov/Places-to-Go/State-Parks/Iowa-State-Parks/Pilot-Knob-State-Park
The floating bog of Dead Man's Lake. Iagen Web Project/ Winnebago County (n.d.). iagenweb.org/winnebago/History/FloatingBog.htm

Hidden Haunted Building

Cichon, B. (2023, November 4). How did Edinburgh Manor in Jones County become a haunted attraction? The *Gazette*. thegazette.com/curious-iowa/curious-iowa-how-did-edinburgh-manor-become-a-haunted-attraction
Edinburgh Manor. The Little House of Horrors. (2022, February 23). thelittlehouseofhorrors.com/edinburgh-manor
History. Edinburgh Manor. (n.d.). edinburghmanor.wixsite.com/edinburgh/history
Leigh, N. (2022, November 19). Edinburgh Manor. Paranormal Investigators of Milwaukee. paranormalmilwaukee.com/locations/edinburgh-manor-iowa
The 9 most haunted places in Iowa. Haunted Rooms America. (2024, March 22). hauntedrooms.com/iowa/haunted-places
True history of Edinburgh Manor: Iowa's haunted insane asylum. Haunted US. (2024, January 20). hauntedus.com/iowa/edinburgh-manor-haunted-asylum/

School's in Session . . . for the Brave!

About Farrar. Farrar Restoration Project (n.d.). hauntingatfarrar.com/about-farrar
Leigh, N. (2020, October 3). Farrar school. Paranormal Investigators of Milwaukee. paranormalmilwaukee.com/locations/haunted-farrar-school-iowa
Ta, L. (2016, October 14). Ghostly things happening in empty school near Des Moines. Des Moines Register. desmoinesregister.com/story/entertainment/2016/10/14/ghostly-things-happening-empty-school-near-des-moines/92050972

Romantic Covered Bridge Has a Dark Side

Bannister, M. (2023). Secret Iowa: A Guide to the Weird, Wonderful, and Obscure. Reedy Press.
Flynn, R. M. (n.d.). The haunted covered bridge in Iowa that will give you chills. Only in Your State. onlyinyourstate.com/experiences/iowa/haunted-covered-bridge-in-ia-2
Pohlen, J. (2005). Oddball Iowa: A guide to some really strange places. Chicago Review Press.
Roseman Covered Bridge. Madison County Tourism. (n.d.). exploremadisoncounty.com/covered_bridges/roseman
This creepy Iowa bridge is haunted by the ghost of an escaped convict. B100. (2017, October 10). b100quadcities.com/this-creepy-iowa-bridge-is-haunted-by-the-ghost-of-an-escaped-convict

Miracle in a Cornfield

Flight 232: It's been 35 years since United Airlines' deadly airplane crash in Iowa. KCCI. (2024, July 19). kcci.com/article/iowa-deadly-airplane-crash-flight-232-sioux-city-35-years/61544759
Flight 232 open house. Mid America Museum of Aviation and Transportation. (n.d.). midamericaairmuseum.org/flight-232-exhibit.html
Jones, E. (2023, July 20). Deadliest plane crash in United Airlines' history killed 112 people. WBAL. wbaltv.com/article/united-flight-232-plane-crash-1989/44589724
McMahan, J., Jones, M., & Phillips, A. (2024, July 19). Friday marks 35 years since Flight 232 crashed at Sioux Gateway Airport. KTIV. ktiv.com/2024/07/19/friday-marks-35-years-since-flight-232-crashed-sioux-gateway-airport
Pohlen, J. (2005). Oddball Iowa: A guide to some really strange places. Chicago Review Press.
Sioux City marks 35th anniversary of Flight 232 crash. Radio Iowa. (2024, July 18). radioiowa.com/2024/07/19/sioux-city-marks-35th-anniversary-of-flight-232-crash

A Lazy Susan Jail

A haunted history of the squirrel cage jail. Council Bluffs Convention and Visitors Bureau. (n.d.). unleashcb.com/blog/a_haunted_history_of_the_squirrel_cage_jail
The haunted (?) Squirrel Cage Jail? Historical Society of Pottawattamie County, Iowa. (n.d.). thehistoricalsociety.org/paranormal/scj-paranormal.html
Welcome to Squirrel Cage Jail. Home. Historical Society of Pottawattamie County, Iowa. (n.d.) thehistoricalsociety.org/museums/squirrel-cage-jail-1.html

Stony Hollow Haunting

13 of Iowa's most haunted spots. Travel Iowa. (n.d.). traveliowa.com/13-of-iowas-most-haunted
Magaraci, K. (n.d.). The mysterious Iowa road you absolutely must drive at least once. Only In Your State. onlyinyourstate.com/trip-ideas/iowa/stony-hollow-road-haunted-ia
Monroe, L. (n.d.). Stay away from Iowa's most haunted street after dark or you may be sorry. Only In Your State. onlyinyourstate.com/experiences/iowa/stony-hollow-road-ia
The 9 most haunted places in Iowa. Haunted Rooms America. (2024, March 22). hauntedrooms.com/iowa/haunted-places

An Unwanted Visitor

Bannister, M. (2023). Secret Iowa: A guide to the weird, wonderful, and obscure. Reedy Press.
Carey, L. (2022, September 30). Revisiting the Van Meter Visitor, as its festival takes shape. The Daily Yonder. dailyyonder.com/visiting-with-the-van-meter-visitor-as-the-festival-takes-shape-this-fall/2021/08/06

Goldfield, R. (n.d.). Van Meter Visitor festival is a paranormal festival in Iowa that will spook you into oblivion. Only In Your State. onlyinyourstate.com/experiences/iowa/paranormal-festival-ia

Register, D. M. (2021, September 24). Half human, half bat: Van Meter remembers a 1903 visit from a winged monster. Des Moines Register. desmoinesregister.com/story/news/2015/07/01/van-meter-remembers-1903-visit-from-winged-monster/29583469

The Van Meter Visitor: Iowa's mysterious winged creature. North American Cryptids (2023, May 20). northamericancryptids.com/van-meter-monster

Chapter 5
Sports Stories

Iowa's Man of Legends

Altenhofen, G. (2022, August 3). Nile Kinnick, famed Iowa football player who died in WWII, to be honored with new documentary. Des Moines Register. desmoinesregister.com/story/entertainment/movies/2022/08/03/nile-kinnick-movie-documentary-honor-iowa-football-player-died-wwii/10187444002

Ironman: The Nile Kinnick story. Iowa History Journal (n.d.). iowahistoryjournal.com/ironman-nile-kinnick-story

Nile Kinnick. Heisman. (2023, July 10). heisman.com/heisman-winners/nile-kinnick

Nile Kinnick. Honor and Remember Nebraska. (2023, August 30). honorandremembernebraska.org/nile-kinnick

Schmidt, D. A. (1996). Iowa pride. Iowa State University Press.

The Cyclone Who Did Big Things

Brunt, C. (2023, November 2). Iowa State's Jack Trice Stadium remains only major college football stadium named for a Black man. AP News. apnews.com/article/jack-trice-iowa-state-02793ce13d1afec4949bc8748ac96b02

History of Iowa state: Alumni—Jack Trice. (n.d.). Iowa State University. historicexhibits.lib.iastate.edu/150/template/trice.html

Morrison, J. (2023, October 6). A century later, Jack Trice's story lives on Iowa Capital Dispatch. iowacapitaldispatch.com/2023/10/06/a-century-later-jack-trices-story-lives-on

Rosengren, J. (n.d.) Jack Trice: Death of a football player, birth of a martyr. johnrosengren.net/jack-trice-death-football-player-birth-martyr

This Black football player was fatally injured during a game. A century later, a college stadium bears his name. Smithsonian. (2023, October 4). smithsonianmag.com/history/this-black-football-player-was-fatally-injured-during-a-game-a-century-later-a-college-stadium-bears-his-name-180982989

The Jack Trice Story. The Jack Trice Commemoration. (n.d.). jacktrice100.com/

From the Grocery Store to the Pros

Kurt Warner. Biography.com (n.d.). biography.com/athletes/a45875740/kurt-warner

Kurt Warner. Pro Football Hall of Fame. (n.d.). profootballhof.com/players/kurt-warner

Kurt Warner. University of Northern Iowa. (n.d.). scholarworks.uni.edu/noteworthy_warner

Ogden, J. R. (2021, December 24). Kurt Warner Loves "American Underdog." but . . . The Gazette. thegazette.com/sports/kurt-warner-loves-american-underdog-but

Sheehan, S. (2023, July 12). Kurt Warner: Biography, net worth, family, top stories. Sportscasting. sportscasting.com/news/kurt-warner-biography-career-net-worth-family-top-stories

Making Swimming an Art Form

Beulah Detwiler Gundling. Coe College (n.d.). public.coe.edu/historyweb/alumni_gundling_beulah_detwiler.htm

Beulah Gundling. International Swimming Hall of Fame. (2024, March 25). ishof.org/honoree/honoree-beulah-gundling

Coffey, J. (2019, October 24). History happenings: Cedar Rapids native, Beulah Gundling, pioneered synchronized swimming. The Gazette. thegazette.com/history/history-happenings-cedar-rapids-native-beulah-gundling-pioneered-synchronized-swimming

Schmidt, D. A. (1996). Iowa pride. Iowa State University Press.

The Caitlin Clark Effect

Allen, G. (2024, March 27). The Caitlin Clark effect: A slam dunk lesson in female empowerment. Forbes. forbes.com/sites/gemmaallen/2024/03/25/the-caitlin-clark-effect-a-slam-dunk-lesson-in-female-empowerment

Crane, P. (2024, August 27). The Caitlin Clark effect: How the rookie phenom is transforming the WNBA. Scripps News. scrippsnews.com/sports/the-caitlin-clark-effect-how-the-rookie-phenom-is-transforming-the-wnba

Miller, K. All about Caitlin Clark. (2024, January 22). womenshealthmag.com/life/a46492597/caitlin-clark-what-to-know

Pastrick, O. (2024, April 9). The Caitlin Clark effect: How the Iowa star is changing women's sports. The Reflector. reflector.uindy.edu/2024/04/10/the-caitlin-clark-effect-how-the-iowa-star-is-changing-womens-sports

The Caitlin Clark effect: Empowering women's sports. Farmers & Merchants. (n.d.). fm.bank/blogs/blog/2024/04/12/the-caitlin-clark-effect--empowering-women's-sports

The Caitlin Clark effect. NCAA.org. (2024, February 15). ncaa.org/news/2024/2/15/media-center-the-caitlin-clark-effect.aspx

Life Is a Balancing Act

About: Shawn Johnson East. Shawnjohnson.com. (n.d.). shawnjohnson.com/thelife

Jordan, E. (2020, November 28). Meet a famous Iowan: Shawn Johnson. The Gazette. thegazette.com/kids-articles/meet-a-famous-iowan-shawn-johnson

Shawn Johnson went to regular school. Gymnastics Coaching (2018, October 10). gymnasticscoaching.com/2018/10/12/shawn-johnson-went-to-regular-school

Stahl, J. (2023, February 16). What Olympic gymnast Shawn Johnson is up to nearly 15 years after winning gold. Des Moines Register. desmoinesregister.com/story/entertainment/2023/02/16/what-iowan-shawn-johnson-andrew-east-doing-now-tv-instagram/69862333007/

Smashing Trains as a Spectator Sport

Crowder, C. (2021, August 10). Head-on train crashes, buying an elephant and other crazy stunts the Iowa State Fair once pulled. Des Moines Register. desmoinesregister.com/story/news/local/columnists/courtney-crowder/2019/08/16/iowa-state-fair-attractions-train-crashes-elephants-plane-crashes-war-shrapnel-cannonball-spectacle/2019050001

Great train crash saved Iowa State Fair. Juicebox Interactive. (2024, January 19). juiceboxinteractive.com/blog/creating-an-iowa-state-fair-spectacle

Justin Franz. (2019, September 15). For 40 years, crashing trains was one of America's favorite pastimes. justinfranz.com/writing/for-40-years-crashing-trains-was-one-of-americas-favorite-pastimes

Most trains wrecked. Guinness World Records. (2021, January 27). guinnessworldrecords.com/world-records/646952-most-trains-wrecked

Inventing the Butterfly

Dave Armbruster. International Swimming Hall of Fame (ISHOF). (2024, March 25). ishof.org/honoree/honoree-dave-armbruster

DesPlanque, T. (n.d.). The University of Iowa: Birthplace of the butterfly stroke. The Daily Iowan. dailyiowan.com/2018/10/11/the-university-of-iowa-birthplace-of-the-butterfly-stroke

Hall of Fame: 2002—Coach Dave Armbruster. American Swimming Coaches Association (n.d.). swimmingcoach.org/page/HOFdavearmbruster

Kieffer, B. (n.d.). Butterfly stroke invented in Iowa pool. Iowa Public Radio. iowapublicradio.org/show/river-to-river/2014-09-25/butterfly-stroke-invented-in-iowa-pool

Schmidt, D. A. (1996). Iowa pride. Iowa State University Press.

Jump Around

George Nissen. Lemelson-MIT. (n.d.). lemelson.mit.edu/resources/george-nissen

Gunnink, A. (2023, March 3). George Nissen and the trampoline. University of Iowa Lichtenberger Engineering Library. blog.lib.uiowa.edu/eng/george-nissen-and-the-trampoline

How the trampoline came to be. Smithsonian (2020, March 5). smithsonianmag.com/innovation/how-trampoline-came-be-180974343/

Kennedy, P. (2012, September 28). Who made that trampoline? New York Times. nytimes.com/2012/09/30/magazine/who-made-that-trampoline.html

Schmidt, D. A. (1996). Iowa pride. Iowa State University Press.

Tarshis, L. (2019, October 1). The history of the trampoline. Scholastic Storyworks. storyworks.scholastic.com/pages/sandbox/100119/the-history-of-the-trampoline.html?language=english

For the Love of Baseball

Cantine-Maxson, S. (1995). New Albin celebrating 150 years since it was first platted. The Standard. waukonstandard.com/articles/2022/07/15/new-albin-celebrating-150-years-it-was-first-platted

Harris "Shooky" Fink. IAGen Web Project. (n.d.). iagenweb.org/boards/allamakee/biographies/index.cgi?read=149880

McGonagle, D.E. (2014, July 29.) Shooky Fink: More than a quarter-century later his legacy remains. Caledonia Argus. hometownsource.com/caledonia/news/local/shooky-fink-more-than-a-quarter-century-later-his-legacy-remains/article_4a7c4507-156f-5308-8f34-6391f5932e52.html

Stewart, L. Shooky Fink Field. PocketSights (n.d.). pocketsights.com/tours/place/Shooky-Fink-Field-16761:1969

Coaching Legends Begins with Being One

Dan Gable. Iowa Wrestling Hall of Fame. (n.d.). iowawrestlinghalloffame.com/inductee/dan-gable

Full Biography. DanGable.com (2020, November 19). dangable.com/bio Klingman, K. (2023, September 11).

National Wrestling Hall of Fame Dan Gable Museum. National Wrestling Hall of Fame. (n.d.). nwhof.org/national-wrestling-hall-of-fame-dan-gable-museum

Puma, M. (n.d.) Gable dominated as wrestler and coach. espn.com/classic/biography/s/Gable_Dan.html

Who is Dan Gable? Learn more about Iowa's iconic wrestling coach. FloWrestling. flowrestling.org/articles/11224692-who-is-dan-gable-learn-more-about-iowas-iconic-wrestling-coach

The Greatest Bike Ride Ever

Explaining the origin of Iowa's iconic bike ride, RAGBRAI. Iowa Local 5 News. youtube.com/watch?v=VcAhKg7QHds

Hamlet, I. (2023, January 29). Brush up on your RAGBRAI history as the ride across Iowa marks its 50th year. Des Moines Register. desmoinesregister.com/story/life/living-well/ragbrai/2023/01/29/explore-ragbrais-history-as-the-ride-founded-in-1973-turns-50/69841467007

Joens, P. (n.d.). New to RAGBRAI? Here's everything rookies need to know before riding across Iowa. Des Moines Register. desmoinesregister.com/story/life/living-well/ragbrai/2022/03/27/ragbrai-2022-route-camping-eating-sleeping-biking-guide-rookie/6706976001

RAGBRAI History: Factoids. RAGBRAI. (2016, November 7). ragbrai.com/about/ragbrai-history-factoids

Riding through history. State Historical Society of Iowa. (n.d.). history.iowa.gov/history/museum/exhibits/riding-through-history

Index